To Deb

From

Keep Praying!!

God Bless

X

# heart2heart

## Contemporary prayers, litanies and liturgies for Christian Worship

### John Birch

**MOORLEY'S** Print & Publishing

© Copyright 2004

British Library Cataloguing in Publication Data.
A catalogue record for this book is available
from the British Library.

ISBN 0 86071 574 4

**MOORLEY'S** Print & Publishing
23 Park Rd., Ilkeston, Derbys DE7 5DA
Tel/Fax: (0115) 932 0643

# Contents

We are growing publishers, adding several new titles to our list each year. We also undertake private publications and commissioned works.

Our range includes:-

**Books of Verse:**
Devotional Poetry
Recitations for Children
Humorous Monologues

**Drama**
Bible Plays
Sketches
Christmas, Passiontide,
    Easter and Harvest Plays
Demonstrations

**Resource Books**
Assembly Material
Songs and Musicals
Children's Addresses
Prayers
Worship and Preaching
Books for Speakers

**Activity Books**
Quizzes
Puzzles
Painting Books

**Church Stationery**
Notice Books
Cradle Roll Certificates
Presentation Labels

**Associated Lists and Imprints**
Cliff College Publishing
Nimbus Press
Headway
Social Workers Christian Fellowship

Please send a stamped addressed envelope (C5 approx 9" x 6") for the current catalogue or consult your local Christian Bookshop who will either stock or be able to obtain Moorleys titles.

# Introduction

In its simplest definition prayer is a conversation between the one who is praying and the one to whom those prayers is directed.

Prayer can take many forms, and encompass the whole range of poetic and literary styles. It can be a cry for help or a cry of joy. It can be a single word or a symphony of prose.

Pope John Paul II is quoted as follows on the difficulty of praying. *"How to pray? This is a simple matter. I would say: Pray any way you like, so long as you do pray."*

Prayers can be individual or corporate, liturgical or extemporary. They can be short or long, simple or complex in language. In fact words are not always necessary, for we have the promise that when words fail us the Spirit will intercede for us with the most intimate prayers of our heart.

What is offered in this book is a collection of prayers and a style of praying which I have found useful within the context of corporate acts of worship, mainly in small gatherings.

Living for some years in Wales and being aware of the interest and influence of the early Celtic Church within this land, it is difficult not to be influenced by the vision and prayer life of the early Christian saints.

To the Celtic Church their God was a personal and loving God totally involved in the whole of the Created world, which He had breathed into existence.

God was with them when they pulled weeds out of their gardens. He was there when they milked their cows; when they gave birth and when they lay down in the darkness of their simple huts in the cold of the evening.

The Celts knew that their God was involved totally in all of His Creation. They held firm to a belief in the incarnation and the knowledge that Jesus Christ lived, died and rose again from death to show the great Love of God for His Creation, and indeed for all of us, His creatures.

Michael Mitton in his excellent book 'Restoring the Woven Cord' talks of the Celts' love of wholeness, and how they wove together the various strands of their faith into a most effective cord for ministry and mission.

Mitton suggests that over the centuries the Church has picked and chosen from these strands, ignoring, losing and then re-discovering lost strands as if they were the most important strand of all.

As a result, the original Cord and the effectiveness of the Church in its mission has become weaker.

The strands of the Celtic cord which Mitton emphasises are holiness, a love of the Bible, the importance of children, community, creation, creativity, death, evangelism, healing and miracles, the Ministry of Women, prayer, prophesy, spiritual warfare and the Wild Goose (the Holy Spirit).

It is my opinion that the early Church in this land was in some ways much closer to the heart of God than our current denominational jumble sale. We can pick and choose as we would sweets in a market stall - there's something for everyone. But the strength of the Church is surely in a weaving together of all the strands of our Christian faith - One Church, One Faith, One Lord.

I started this introduction by stating that at its simplest prayer is a conversation, and conversations are rarely one-sided. Within our time of prayer needs to be the silence that enables God to contribute. David Adam says of silence 'It is not an empty time but a God-filled time.'

*'Let the words of my mouth and the meditation of my heart*
*Be acceptable in Your sight, O Lord, my strength and my Redeemer'*

*(Psalm 19:14)*

John Birch, Kidwelly, Wales 2003

# Worship in the Early Church

If we look at two early accounts of the Church at worship we can begin to get a feel for the foundations of our own denominational style.

Pliny was governor of the Roman province of Bithynia, and in the year 112 AD wrote to the Emperor asking for advice on what to do about troublesome Christians.

It was the practice of these Christians '...to sing antiphonally a song to Christ as a god, and to bind themselves on oath... to commit no theft, murder, adultery, not to break their word, not to deny possession of something entrusted to them... to disperse and then reassemble to share a common meal together...'

From this we may deduce that the early Christian Church used song and the Ten Commandments within their times of worship together.

From approximately forty years later comes an account from the Christian Justin Martyr. He describes the format of an early gathering of Christians.

There are readings from the Word, followed by a sermon. The people would then stand for prayer, after which would be the sharing of the kiss of peace. Bread and wine were shared, and prayers said by the president. Justin uses the term 'Eucharist' (meaning 'thanksgiving') to describe the sharing of sacrament and prayer.

There are some lovely prayers that have survived from the fledgling Church. In the *Didache* (a first or second century Christian treatise on Church practice) comes this prayer.

*'Just as the bread broken was scattered on the hills, then was gathered and became one, so let Your Church be gathered from all the ends of the earth into Your kingdom, for Yours is the glory and power through all ages.'*

As we pass into the third century and beyond we find descriptions for various acts of worship. Hippolytus gives us a liturgy for the Eucharist to be used during the consecration of a bishop, which is similar in style to our modern forms of liturgy, with familiar responses such as 'The Lord be with you', 'And with your Spirit'.

Although Justin Martyr's description of a Christian gathering contains echoes of our more familiar 'service of word and sacrament' there is very little known about the 'service of the word' (sometimes known as the synaxis) in New Testament times.

Later evidence suggests influence from the synagogues, in the form of readings and prayers. In Colossians 3:16 we read that the Church was encouraged to '...sing psalms, hymns and spiritual songs' and in Corinthians we have descriptions of the gifts used within the Church - prophesy, ecstatic utterance, interpretation, revelations and teaching.

For the apostle Paul, the most important consideration seems to have been that Christians '...present your bodies as a living sacrifice, holy and acceptable to God, which is your spiritual worship.'

From the evidence of Scripture and the early centuries of the Christian Church the sharing of bread and wine (the Eucharist) seems to have been at the heart of Christian worship. This sacred element together with the reading of the Word, songs, sermon and prayer seem to have been the foundation upon which most of our modern styles of worship have built.

One commentator has stated that all worship should be 'eucharistic' in that it should centre on the cross of Christ, have at its heart thanksgiving, allow for all to participate and have a sense of sacred drama as truth is proclaimed through actions.

# Prayers in the early Church

These are examples of prayers handed down to us from the first centuries of the Christian Church.

Look upon us, O Lord,
and let all the darkness of our souls vanish before
              the beams of thy brightness.
Fill us with holy love, and open to us the treasures of thy wisdom.
All our desire is known unto thee,
              therefore perfect what thou hast begun,
and what thy Spirit has awakened us to ask in prayer.
We seek thy face,
turn thy face unto us and show us thy glory.
Then shall our longing be satisfied,
and our peace shall be perfect.                    *(Augustine, 354 - 430)*

We beseech thee, Master, to be our helper and protector.
Save the afflicted among us;
have mercy on the lowly; raise up the fallen;
appear to the needy; heal the ungodly;
restore the wanderers of thy people;
feed the hungry;
ransom our prisoners; raise up the sick; comfort the faint-hearted.
                              *(Clement of Rome, 1st Century)*

O Lord, who hast mercy upon all, take away from me my sins,
and mercifully kindle in me the fire of thy Holy Spirit.
Take away from me the heart of stone, and give me a heart of flesh, a heart
to love and adore thee, a heart to delight in thee, to follow and to enjoy
thee, for Christ's sake.                    *(Ambrose of Milan, c 339-97)*

Deep peace of the running wave to you,
Deep peace of the flowing air to you,
Deep peace of the quiet earth to you,
Deep peace of the shining stars to you,
Deep peace of the Son of Peace to you, for ever.
                              *(Source unknown - early Scottish)*

O good shepherd, seek me out,
and bring me home to thy fold again.
Deal favourably with me according to thy good pleasure,
till I may dwell in thy house all the days of my life,
and praise thee for ever and ever with them that are there.

*(Jerome, c 342 - 420)*

Alone with none but thee, my God,
I journey on my way.
What need I fear, when thou art near O king of night and day?
More safe am I within thy hand
Than if a host did round me stand.

*(Columba, c.521 - 97)*

Lord, thou hast given us thy Word
for a light to shine upon our path;
grant us so to meditate on that Word, and to follow its teaching,
that we may find in it the light, that shines more and more,
until the perfect day; through Jesus Christ our Lord.

*(Jerome, c 342 - 420)*

May God the Father bless us; may Christ take care of us;
the Holy Ghost enlighten us all the days of our life.
The Lord be our defender and keeper of body and soul
both now and for ever, to the ages of ages.

*(Æthelwold c 908-984)*

# The Components of our Prayer

'The Lord said:
I heard your prayer and what you asked me to do'

*(1 Kings 9:3)*

If we are going to be creative in our prayer time then I do not feel that there should be too many hard and fast rules about the format and content. We are all individuals with our own thoughts about style and content, and this 'individuality ' can bring a freshness and vitality into a time spent talking and listening to God.

A structured prayer time is more familiar in some denominations than others, who perhaps prefer extemporary prayer or an element of congregational participation by way of a time of 'open prayer'. Both are equally valid.

However, within the context of our collective worship there are certain elements that it would seem right to include, in order that our prayers are not seen to be too narrow in their aspirations.

These can be represented by the acronym A.C.T.S.

(i) **ADORATION**: Our prayer of adoration is one that is centred entirely on God. It is our expression of praise for all that God is - His holiness, majesty, love and greatness.

It's that mountaintop experience of being in the presence of the Creator of all that you see around you, or sitting through a truly wonderful performance of a sacred work which has transported your soul to another plain. Perhaps you see what I'm trying to explain?

Adoration comes from the heart, from our emotions; it's an expression of our inmost feelings.

(ii) CONFESSION: An awareness of God's presence within our worship naturally leads on to a feeling of our own unworthiness. In confession we acknowledge what we are and ask for forgiveness.

If these prayers are part of an act of public worship then it is appropriate to express the Christian conviction that we all share in the sin of humankind.

Any prayer of confession should properly express our belief that God offers the promise of forgiveness.

(iii) THANKSGIVING: Often lost within the package of prayer offered within worship is thanksgiving. It gets confused with adoration or simply ignored as prayers focus on intercession.

It is only right and proper that we should thank God for all that He has done. For the beauty of this world which He created, for the birth, life, death and resurrection of Jesus Christ, the promise of the Holy Spirit, His continuing creativity in the world today and for the Church - His body here on earth.

(iv) SILENCE: Silence is important, in that it allows us time to digest all that has been said through prayer. It gives us precious time within worship to let our hearts talk and our mouths stay silent.

As David Adam says 'It is not an empty time but a God-filled time when we open ourselves up to him.

A time of silence enables those worshipping to 'own' the prayers and make them their own. It also allows for active participation for those who would not feel able to contribute vocally.

Within the context of an act of worship there is often time set aside for intercessory prayer, and this naturally arises as a response to the hearing of God's word. When we pray for others, we are adding our pleas to Christ's perfect prayer for the whole world.

'Christ Jesus ... is at the right hand of God and is also interceding for us.'

# Creation

'Creation by its very existence witnesses to
and proclaims its creaturehood,
it proclaims that it has been produced.'

*George Florovsky*

'Jesus chose the way and the lifestyle of the storyteller,
the parable-maker who fashions a new creation
out of the holy materials of the only creation
that we all share in common.'

*Matthew Fox*

'Faith makes the world what it truly is,
the creation of God.'

*Gerard Ebeling*

Every creature, every plant,
every rock and grain of sand
proclaims the glory of its Creator;
worships through colour, shape
scent and form.
A multi-sensory song of praise.
Creator God, may we join
with the whole of Your creation
in praising You, our Creator,
through the fragrance
and melody of our lives.

Creator God,
on windswept beaches
Your saints of old
held their hands up to You.
In wonder and amazement
felt Your power through the roar
of wind and surf, and
exposed to the elements
felt a unity
with the One
who had created all things.
This world does not often allow us
such intimacy, Father
we are crowded out
by circumstances of our own choosing;
seeking fellowship with each other
rather than with You.
Forgive our unwillingness
to follow in the footsteps of Your saints;
to meet You in the solitude of Your creation
Forgive our unwillingness
to get our feet wet.

After the storm
a rainbow skilfully painted
from the spectrum of colours
contained in Your glorious palette.
Warm colours encircling us
embracing this earth
with a promise.
A reminder of Your covenant
with all of Your creation.
Such love;
eternal and everlasting.
Thank You, Creating God
for the beauty of the rainbow
and the beauty of Your love:
For all that You have made
and are going to make.

This world
Your creation
Rolled into a sphere
Packaged in sunshine
Gift-wrapped in love
Given to us
Thank You!

In the beginning, Lord I was alone
Like the earth
before Your Spirit moved over the waters.
I was formless and empty
and darkness filled the depths of my heart.
Then, it was as if You declared
'Let there be Light'
and out of the darkness
I began to see hope
like a shimmering ray of love
breaking through the parting clouds
at the conclusion of the night.
In the beginning, Lord I was alone
but when I saw You in the light
I was no longer afraid.
You held out Your hand
and though I had a choice
I had no choice
because to refuse
was to embrace again the darkness.
In the beginning, Lord I was alone
Now I feel again a part of Your creation
loved, wanted, needed, family.
In the light of Your presence
I hold out my heart that others
might glimpse through it Your reflection
and be drawn from the darkness
that I once embraced
into the light of Your sunrise
the brightness of Your face

The Lord reigns, let the earth be glad:

**ALL:**    **Let the distant shores rejoice**

By Your word all things were created
each in its allotted space and time.
You breathed life through Your Spirit
and in the whisper of the wind we are reminded

of Your Spirit's continual presence.

The Lord reigns, let the earth be glad.

**ALL:**    **Let the distant shores rejoice**

The whole of creation declares Your glory, Lord.
A symphony of sound and colour surround us
if we will for a moment stand
with eyes and ears attuned.

The Lord reigns, let the earth be glad.

**ALL:**    **Let the distant shores rejoice**

The whole of humankind declares Your glory, Lord.
Each precious son or daughter a unit of love
in the currency of Your family.

The Lord reigns, let the earth be glad.

**ALL:**    **Let the distant shores rejoice**

Now in our worship we declare Your glory, Lord.
Proclaim Your Kingdom to the ends of the earth
Your love to the highest mountain
Your forgiveness to the depths of the sea.

The Lord reigns, let the earth be glad.

**ALL:**    **Let the distant shores rejoice**

This world is not the accomplishment
of a moment of Your time, Lord,
that we can see clearly.
Those rugged cliffs
thrust from the depths of the sea,
filled with the evidence of the past,
were not created in the blinking of an eye.
The diamond's hardness did not come suddenly.
This is the work of an infinite patience
the creation of something
of which its creator could be pleased.

And now Lord, this infinite patience
this creative love is directed towards us
formed as we are from the very elements
of the world in which we live.
Your creative Spirit still at work, tireless, ceaseless
endlessly creating in our hearts
the image of Your likeness.
The only difference being
the diamond had no choice
in whether it would be transformed
into such beauty.

The warmth of the sun's embrace
the gentle breeze swept in by incoming tide
The rhythm of seasons
of new birth, death and recreation
All these speak so clearly of Your love,
Your power and Your beauty.
All are expressions of Your creativity
and more importantly of Yourself!
As an artist might share his personality
within each brushstroke
so within the myriad colours
of a butterfly's wing
You share the exuberance of Your love.
That we can glimpse You
within creation is a beautiful thought
but also tells us that You desire to be seen
to be found; and known.
Open our eyes, Lord
as we walk through this world
feel the wind and sunshine
see the majesty of Your creation
unfolding before our eyes
Help us to see You

# Seasons

'Grace grows better in the winter.'

*Samuel Rutherford*

'There will be seasons of loneliness and sadness, and it seems to me
as it was so in the case of all the people we read of in the Bible.
Our Lord distinctly told His disciples to expect it to be so
and even experienced this sorrow of heart himself…
so I don't learn that I ought exactly to wish it otherwise.'

*John Coleridge Patteson*

'It is always springtime in the heart that loves God.'

*Jean-Baptiste Marie Vianney*

Creator God
at the start of this New Year
when thoughts turn again to beginnings:
starting afresh
new leaves
and turning skeletons free from cupboards
be with us
as we gaze into the distance of fresh mission grounds
of hopes and dreams, opportunities for service
challenges and uncertainties.
Take our fears and turn them into strengths.
Take our lack of faith
and empower us through the Spirit
who breathes life into this world;
whose presence is reflected
in the icy chill of winter's breath
as well as the comforting warmth
of a summer breeze.
Walk with us into this New Year of opportunity

# Lent

Forty days alone,
a wilderness of thoughts -
tempting and inviting thoughts
which could so easily have distracted You
from Your task, Your mission, Your vision.
Yet You emerged, stronger and more attuned
to all that had to be done despite a time constraint
that to our eyes would have seemed hopeless.
We too live in stressful times.
Demands are made of our time
that leave so little for the important things of life.
We are easily distracted
in the wilderness of our lives
by every call to go this way or that
to turn stone to bread
leap from mountains
and do all that would keep us from the truth.
We listen to the voices of this world
and ignore the one who endured all this
and so much more
and emerged triumphant
that we might not have to suffer so.
Forgive us, Father
when we get distracted from our task.
Forgive us those times when we try
to be all things to all men
and fail to be anything to anyone.

It is customary, Lord to give something up
during the season of Lent.
What would You have me do without?
I who have so much:
Chocolate? - Cream cakes?
Cigarettes? - Sweets? - Swearing?
The list is endless
and I could give up all those things

for the span of 40 days
quite easily and almost painlessly.
But what difference would it make
other than making me feel 'holier'
than my friend who makes no such sacrifice?

What would You have me do without?
I who have so much:
Selfishness? - Conceit?
Envy? - Pride?
I fear before I ask
that the answer might be 'yes'
and the giving up
would be all too real, Lord.
It would be difficult; painful; sacrificial
a real cross to carry for 40 days
and more?

## Easter

Blest are You, Lord Jesus who came to us a little child
one of us, flesh and blood to share in our humanity
For God so loved the world

**ALL:**   **That all might have eternal life**

Blest are You, Lord Jesus who came to us as carpenter
and yet in whose creative hands a world was fashioned
For God so loved the world

**ALL:**   **That all might have eternal life**

Blest are You, Lord Jesus who came to us as fisherman
and yet pointed to a harvest that was yet to come
For God so loved the world

**ALL:**   **That all might have eternal life**

Blest are You, Lord Jesus who came to us as teacher
and opened eyes to truths that only
the poor could understand
For God so loved the world

**ALL:** **That all might have eternal life**

Blest are You, Lord Jesus who came to us as healer
and opened hearts to the reality of wholeness
For God so loved the world

**ALL:** **That all might have eternal life**

Blest are You, Lord Jesus who came to us as prophet, priest and
king
and yet humbled himself
to take our place upon the cross
For God so loved the world

**ALL:** **That all might have eternal life**

Blest are You, Lord Jesus who came to us as servant
and revealed to us the extent of His Father's love
for human kind
For God so loved the world

**ALL:** **That all might have eternal life**

Blest are You, Lord Jesus, who rose
from the ignominy of a sinner's death
to the triumph of a Saviour's resurrection
For God so loved the world

**ALL:** **That all might have eternal life**

God so loved the world that He gave His only Son
for the sake of me
and You
and other sinners too
God so loved the world
Blest are You Lord Jesus, our Saviour and Redeemer.

# Pentecost

Pentecost is indeed a time of celebration.
A celebration that two thousand years of oppression
have failed to extinguish.
God of Pentecost

**ALL:** **Keep alight Your fire in our hearts**

It's a celebration that remembers the surprise
on the faces of those gathered on that first Pentecost
when they heard Your word speaking to their hearts.
God of Pentecost

**ALL:** **Keep alight Your fire in our hearts**

It's a celebration that remembers the generations of disciples
who have carried the torch of Your flame
to the furthest corners of this world in which we live.
God of Pentecost

**ALL:** **Keep alight Your fire in our hearts**

It's a celebration that remembers the warm feeling
in our hearts when we first heard You
speaking directly to us
through Your word and Your messengers.
God of Pentecost

**ALL:** **Keep alight Your fire in our hearts**

It's a celebration that not only looks back
but looks forward to all that You are going to do
as we take up the flame of Your Spirit and hold it aloft.
God of Pentecost

**ALL:** **Keep alight Your fire in our hearts**

When was the last time that we heard the wind
of Your Spirit roar through this place?
When was the last time Your fire lit up this room?
When was the last time we took You at Your word
and met together in expectation

23

of Your Spirit filling this place
and these lives with Your Glory and Power?
Lord, You challenge us with Pentecost.
Do we believe that this was a once in eternity experience
never to be repeated?
That the Holy Spirit was poured out
on Your followers for a single purpose
and ended His work at that instant?
If so, then maybe that is why the Church
seems so powerless in this age;
helpless when faced with the needs
both spiritual and physical that we see in the world.
Lord, as we meet together and celebrate once again
the memory of that first Pentecost
may it be for us as it was then:
A moment of empowerment
an awareness of Your Glory in this dark world -
a life changing experience.

Father
Son
Spirit
Holy Trinity
made known to us
through revelation
through experience
and Your Word.
Father
Son
Spirit
Holy Trinity
Alive in hearts
and minds and souls
and manifest
throughout Your world

Father
Son
Spirit
Holy Trinity
Comforter of souls
Defender of the weak
Advocate and power
in life and death
Father
Son
Spirit
Holy Trinity
we praise You,
worship
and adore You

We light a candle
and enjoy the flickering light
the fragrance and warmth it creates.
But without the spark that ignites
there will be no flame
Without the wax, the source of power,
the wick will not burn
Without the flame there will be no fragrance
no warmth, no light.
And so with us, Lord.
You are the catalyst that ignites us
and the fuel that sustains us.
You fill us with Your fragrance
as You enter our lives.
You empower us
to carry Your flame in our hearts.
To be the fragrance, warmth
and light of Your love in this dark world.

## Trinity Sunday

Glorious Trinity
Make Your presence known in this place
through our worship
our prayer
the reading of Your Word.
Father, Son, Holy Spirit
within whose unity lies all that is You:-
perfect love, justice, peace and power.
As we gather here today
Your body, Your church
throughout this world
fill our outstretched hearts with Your spirit
encircle us with Your love.
Make Yourself known to us in new ways
exciting ways, challenging ways
Empower us
Inspire us
Glorious Trinity.

1)     Your Spirit

2)     Your Breath

3)     Your Power

1)     Be with us

2)     Reside in us

3)     Revive us

**All)**     **Fill our hearts and minds**

1)     With the knowledge of Your love

2)     With the assurance of Your word

3)     With the power to proclaim

**All)**     **The Good News of the Kingdom.**

Spirit of life

**ALL:**     **Fill our emptiness with Your fullness**

Spirit of power

**ALL:**     **Stir our hearts afresh**

Spirit of love

**ALL:**     **Touch us, and through us, our neighbour**

Spirit of Creativity

**ALL:**     **Enable and empower the gifts You have given**

Spirit of Eternity

**ALL:**     **Draw us ever deeper into Your Kingdom.**

# Advent

In this season of expectation

**We prepare to welcome Christ Jesus, Messiah**

Into the bustle of our lives
and the hard to find moments of solitude

**We prepare to welcome Christ Jesus, Messiah**

Into our homes and situations
along with friends and families

**We prepare to welcome Christ Jesus, Messiah**

Into our hearts, and those often hidden parts of our lives

**We prepare to welcome Christ Jesus, Messiah**

For beneath the surface of Your story
is an inescapable fact
You entered this world
as vulnerable as any one of us
in order to nail that vulnerability to the cross.
Our fears, our insecurities and our sins
all that can separate us from God
exchanged by Your Grace for Love.
We cannot comprehend the reasoning
only marvel that Salvation comes to us
through a baby born in a stable,
and reaches out to a world in need.

In this season of anticipation

**We prepare to welcome Christ Jesus, Messiah.**

# Christmas

The joy of discovery, that moment when hope
and expectation were gloriously met
by the illumination of one bright star.
We cannot imagine
what words were spoken by visitors,
or if first impressions left them somewhat confused.
Messiah, Saviour, a King born in the barest of palaces.
Yet they saw and fell down on their knees in adoration.
Lord, they saw You and knew whom they had met.
As we meet around crib, candle or advent wreath
draw us into that stable in our imagination.
In the quiet moments of prayer this Christmas,
that brief oasis from the bustle of the world,
bring alive to us the smell of the hay,
the sound of the animals,
the cry of a baby.
Draw us close to our Saviour, Messiah and King
as we offer; not Gold, Myrrh or Frankincense
but the gift of our lives
the only offering we can bring.

What was it in that natal star,
pre-eminent in the night-time sky
that stirred the hearts and imaginations
of those magi from the east?
Was it colour, brightness, conjunction or more?
A still small voice - whispering
in the darkness of the world:
'This is the sign that will proceed the birth
of He who fulfils the prophets' words.'
That still small voice
which whispers still to our conscience and soul
still leads - if we will but follow
to the stable door.

There were thousands of babies
born that day
all helpless; dependent
needful of love, warmth and sustenance
some no doubt did not survive
to see another dawn
their tiny light extinguished
through lack of appropriate care.
Some would grow up to be kings
queens, leaders of men.
Others slaves, prostitutes, beggars
murderers and thieves.
Most, however would live ordinary lives
among ordinary people - and live and die
whilst the world scarce noticed their existence.
But not You
Who rose from the ordinary to the extraordinary
from stable to cross - and beyond
whilst the world tried its best to ignore You
and failed!

## The Year

When You created this world
and all that exists upon it
and breathed Your life-giving breath
upon those first organisms,
did You get a thrill
as that first flower bloomed?
Was it exactly as You had designed it?
We buy our seeds in packets
drawn by the promise of a photograph or drawing,
aided by books and TV programmes
and yet still marvel
when those first seeds germinate,
grow and burst into flower.
You had no such help in planning Your garden
and yet achieved perfection.

I look at any wayside bank
and see a herbaceous border
balanced in size and colour.
I see the broad sweep of a hillside
and the subtle shades of green
transformed through the seasons
to give a breadth of colour
that any garden designer
would be proud to have created.
Thank You for Springtime, Creator God
and for the inspiration it provides to me
a gardener.

Springtime!
Your message of hope
to a world tiring of winter's starkness,
longing for that first crocus
to push through snow's icy blanket
and spread its leaves
like arms outstretched
to its creator.
Springtime!
Our yearly reminder, if we needed one,
that to a world that was dark and cold;
a world devoid of love's sweet warmth
You sent Your Son
To break through sin's icy blanket.
Arms outstretched on a cross
he brought us
hope
Thank You!

There is real wisdom, Lord, in the adage
'It is always Springtime in the heart that loves God.'
Springtime is a season of optimism and hope
and the Christian lives a faith centred on hope.
Winter, with its cold and dark days has gone
just as Good Friday has passed to Easter and beyond.
We live a resurrection life
reflected in the new life springing up around us.
Thank You, Lord for the hope that You bring;
the renewal that You bring
both to this world and to our hearts and lives.

Under the warmth of the summer sun
the world awakes and blossoms
into every imaginable colour.
You created a garden for us to enjoy
and within it planted
the most magical of flower and trees.
You needed no horticultural training
to plan Your colour scheme;
no gardening expert to recommend variety or design.
Your garden is perfect; its colours harmonious
its scale immense; spoilt only by the clumsiness
of those who tend it.
Creator God, who breathed this world into being
who is discernible within the harmony of nature
the perfection of a butterfly's wing
the grandeur of a mountain range
the soaring eagle and humming bird.
Thank You for this world which You have created
Thank You for summer sun
which reminds us that Your creative breath
is still alive and active.
Thank You for the warmth of Your love
sustaining this world
Your garden.

So many shades of gold:
Autumn
Another miracle we take for granted.
Another expression of the artist's vision:
The blending of the autumn hues
with the setting sun.
Warm.
Comforting!
Perfect!!
Thank You for autumn, Lord.

The Church is full of people
in the Autumn of their years.
Some have led colourful lives;
leaves bronzed and golden
through exposure to the elements;
their appearance the centre of attention.
Others have been exposed
to more extreme conditions
branches bowed and scarred.
Some go unnoticed,
yet stand tall and steadfast
against wind and rain.
All have a story to tell
all can offer support and shelter
for saplings which grow beneath
their leafy canopy.

There is a winter in all of our lives,
a chill and darkness that makes us yearn
for days that have gone,
or put our hope in days yet to be.
Father God, You created seasons for a purpose.
Spring is full of expectation:
buds breaking; frosts abating and an awakening
of creation before the first days of summer.
Now the sun gives warmth and comfort to our lives
reviving aching joints;
bringing colour, new life
and crops to fruiting.
Autumn gives nature space
to lean back, relax and enjoy the fruits of its labour
mellow colours in sky and landscape
as the earth prepares to rest.
Then winter, cold and bare
as nature takes stock
rests, unwinds, sleeps until the time is right.
An endless cycle
and yet a perfect model.
We need a winter in our lives:
a time of rest, a time to stand still;
a time to reacquaint ourselves
with the faith in which we live.
It is only then that we can draw strength
from the One in whom we are rooted;
take time to grow and rise through the darkness
into the warm glow of Your springtime
to blossom and flourish
bring colour and vitality into this world
Your garden.
Thank You Father
for the seasons of our lives.

# The World

'The whole world ought to be regarded as the visible part
of a universal and continuing sacrament, and all man's
activities as a sacramental, divine communion.'

*Dumitru Staniloae*

'Come to the world!
Yes, God the Creator, come!
Things are not as You created them
in the beginning,
Come, God, for it is Your help
We need in the world.'

*Ikoli Harcourt Whyte (Nigerian writer)*

'Our divisions prevent our neighbours from
hearing the Gospel as they should.'

*Pope John Paul II*

'To see God is not to see anything extraordinary
but to see ordinary things as they really are.'

*Lawrence Freeman (English Benedictine)*

This world I live in
this town I live in
this street I live in
this house I live in
may each be the focus of my prayer.
Those I live with
those I rub shoulders with
those I work with
those I don't get on with
may each be the focus of my prayer.
Those who laugh
those who cry
those who hurt
those who hide
may each be the focus of my prayer.
Prayers centred less on self
and more on others
less on my circumstances
more on the needs of others.
May my life be likewise centred
less on self and more on You
and through You to the world
in which I live and move.

It's all in the touch
the touch of love - the touch of healing
the touch of compassion
the touch of reassurance
the touch that says, 'You are special,
wanted, held in high regard'.
It's all in that touch
that very special touch - the touch You give through us
who reach out to those in need
to those who need to know.
Help us to be channels of Your touch
in this dark world
to bring Your love;
healing; compassion
and reassurance
to a world that knows none of these.

There is comfort in the warmth of a hug.
Security
in a reassuring hand on shoulder.
Confidence
in the firm grip of a handshake.
Something passes from giver to receiver
and mysteriously returns with interest.
Yet in a world which worries about values
and investment rates
and the volatility of currencies
so little attention is shown to this simple fact.
The things that are rated of value
in this world are temporary,
fluctuating with the uncertainty
of the Stock Market.
Love meanwhile is constant
its value increasing each time it is given away.
This, Lord is the Investment Trust
of which You are in control.
Thank You that this is one
we can indeed rely upon.

Saints of days long gone
standing on seashore and mountain top
considered the might of the elements
that You had created:
the roar of the wind and waves
the constancy of the tides and seasons.
To them, Lord, it was evidence enough
that Your creative Spirit was still empowering
this fragile world, encircling their lives
as the very wind and mist that swirled around them.
We have so little time to contemplate this world
and complain when wind and rain
conspire to spoil our day.
Yet in doing so we often fail to gain the comfort
and reassurance that Your saints felt in their isolation.
We forget that it was Your creative breath
that set this universe in motion
and still moves across the world.
Not always predictably - but there to be seen and felt
there to offer the comfort and reassurance
of a God who is constant and eternal.
Thank You, Creator God
for the constancy and ample evidence
of Your love for this world.

Time is something I have so little of, Lord
But then You know that I am a busy person
Busy for You, Lord - doing Your work.
It's tiring, very tiring
and at times I wish it were not so
that I had time for others - for myself
for You...

> *'Son, you have all the time in the world - and beyond.*
> *You give so much and yet leave no time for receiving.*
> *That's not how it's meant to be.*
> *It should not be you striving to do My work.*
> *It should properly be Me doing My work through you*
> *There is a difference, you know!'*

In Your time, Lord, in Your time.
Take the imperfect that is me
and create
the person that I could be.
In Your time, Lord, in Your time.

It is not ours to know
the time or place
when You will return.
We have enough to concern us
in these present times
in the day to day business
of living.
But one thing is certain
of this I am sure
we are all a part of history
and history has a purpose
an end point
a destination
and we should live our lives
as if that destination
is ours also.
Lives lived with purpose:
watchful,
prepared,
in expectation.
For if the time is hidden
it may catch us unawares
our temples full
of unwashed linen
dirt and debris.
Perhaps we'd better
get the dustpan out, Lord
and do some unseasonal
spring cleaning!

Thank You Father for the selfless giving of time.
For those often quiet saints who do not argue their theology loudly
engage in lengthy debates over complex doctrinal issues
or make their presence felt within the hallowed space
of Church Council meetings but simply get on with doing
the business - visiting the sick, the aged
and the lonely
a shoulder to cry on, a listening ear
and the reassurance of one who cares.
Thank You Father for all those quiet saints
who live their faith through their lives
in a world that often forgets
that You were never too busy to listen
never too busy to minister to needs
never too engrossed in work
to bring hope and wholeness into lives.
Thank You Father, for Your quiet saints.

Lord God, help us to love those whom we find it difficult to love.
Give us a heart that reaches out to those we would otherwise ignore.
Give us the strength not to cross on the other side of the road
but to play the part of the Samaritan.
This will not be easy, Lord.
It is not in our nature.
We spread our love thinly among those we can relate to
those who share our values and those who do not threaten
our comfortable lifestyle.
It's not easy, Lord and on our own we shall fail.
But with Your help all things are possible.
You led the way and it is Your example that we look to.
You turned the values of this world upside down.
Do the same with us, Lord.
Help us live the reality of Your Love.

Life is stressful, Father.
Every second of our time controlled precisely
whether by work or play:
'Must go there' 'Must do this'
'Must watch that' 'Must buy one of those'
'Must achieve something'
'Must be loved' 'Must feel wanted'
'Must do more' 'Must win'
'Must… must… must…'
Father, You gave us limited hours within each day
for work and play
and balanced them by the allocation of night and day
and provision of the Sabbath.
It is our choice to push the boundaries
of what You consider reasonable
and live our lives to the limits - and get stressed
and unwell.
Bring us back to simplicity of living, Father,
when what matters is not 'must' or 'more'
but 'maybe' and 'in all good time'.
Give us the time to reassess our lives, our worth,
and our responsibilities to ourselves and others.

Can we really move mountains with a mustard seed of faith?
It seems rather a difficult task.
Could we maybe start with a molehill and work our way up gradually?
But that's not the way it works, is it, Lord?
So often You challenge us with the mountain when we feel so unprepared
and unequipped for the task.
It's then that we have to put self aside - and fear - and pride
and cling tightly to Your hand.
It is only then that we really feel the warmth of Your touch,
the certainty of Your love, the power of Your presence.
It is only then that our faith begins to grow
and we begin to see our real potential.

> Thank You, Heavenly Father
> for mountains
> and mustard seeds.

If we had a fraction of the faith in You that You have in us
then this world would be transformed, Lord.
If we showed a fraction of the love that You show to us
then this world would be transformed, Lord
If we possessed a fraction of the patience that You display with us
then this world would be transformed, Lord.
If we shared just a portion of the blessings that we have received from You
then this world would be transformed, Lord.
If we showed as much trust in others as You have shown in us
then this world would be transformed, Lord.
If we claimed just a fraction of the power You promised to Your Church
then this world would be transformed, Lord.
Transform us first, Lord, that we might transform this world
through Your love and Your power.

＊＊＊

From my comfortable armchair, I put the world to rights
solve ancient disputes over territory
find sensible ways to bring peace and harmony
to a world desensitised to violence and hatred
settle moral and ethical dilemmas over embryo research
bring an end to terrorism by bringing all the parties together
to take part in a well tempered discussion.
From my comfortable armchair I control the world
through remote connection to my television screen.
My condemnation of all that is wrong and my solutions
to the problems of this world seem eminently sensible.
There must be many more like me, Lord
and yet this world is torn in pieces by division.
I am a part of that division, Lord - because my voice is only heard
within the walls of my living room.
You overturned the stalls of the moneylenders in the temple,
shouted out Your condemnation; Your righteous anger.
I have my comfortable armchair.
You faced every challenge up-front never turning away.
I have my remote control
and give myself the choice of changing channels.
There's room for improvement in my life, Lord
before I engage with the world.

Loving God, we see all around us the evidence of Your love
and Your loving provision for our needs.
And yet on our television screens
our newspapers and on the streets of our towns and cities
we see people who have so few of life's basic essentials:
clean water, food and shelter.
This is wrong, we know that in our hearts.
You love all of humankind, not just the ones
that history has placed in the so-called developed world.
Loving God, grant a spirit of responsibility
to those in positions of power;
a conscience that sees inequality
and wants to do something about it.
And Lord, include us for we have become immune
to the suffering of others.

For those who bring hope
where there is none
love where there is hatred
peace where there is war
sustenance where there is hunger
water where there is drought
and comfort where there is sadness
bless them Lord Jesus
whether they be Christian, Muslim
no faith or any faith.
For all love has its source in You
and every act of selfless giving
brings a smile to Your face.

When I talk of neighbour
I mean the family next door
whom I might or might not get on with.
When You talk of neighbour
You extend our neighbourhood to the whole world,
to all kinds of people;
the old, the young,
the good and the bad,
those from different social
or ethnic groups.
I see them on my TV screen and just know
that I could not get on with them
if they happened to move in next door.
But then, that is Your challenge to us, isn't it?
To do as You did.
To extend the hand of love
Unconditionally
No strings or prejudice attached.
I can't do that Lord, it is not in my nature.
But I am convinced
that You can do it through me.

# Healing and Forgiveness

'It is not on our forgiveness any more than on our goodness that the world's healing hinges, but on us. When He tells us to love our enemies, He gives, along with the command, the love itself.'

*Corrie ten Boom*

'Hear further, O man, of the work of resurrection going on in you, even though you were unaware of it. For perhaps you have sometimes fallen sick, and lost flesh, and strength, and beauty; but when you once more received mercy and healing from God, you regained flesh and appearance and also recovered your strength.'

*Theophilus of Antioch (d.180)*

'If we really know Christ as our Saviour our hearts are broken and cannot be hard, and we cannot refuse forgiveness.'

*David Martyn Lloyd-Jones*

'Forgiveness is not an occasional act, it is a permanent attitude.'

*Martin Luther King Jnr*

Father God, when we look
into the brightness of Your radiance;
the light that blinds, the light that illuminates
each dusty corner of our everyday lives,
it is hard to feel anything but embarrassment
as we stand, kneel or sit in Your house
sing Your praises
say 'Amen' 'Alleluia'.
Something, that still small voice, whispers insistently
in our ears 'There's unfinished business here'.
And we know it means cleaning out those corners,
vacuuming out the dust and debris of the past,
throwing away all that we have clung to,
derived undue comfort from,

to start afresh
clean
refreshed
pure
ready to do Your will.
Help us to make that effort
to rid our lives of all that is unclean;
so that Your light may not be obscured
by the darkness of our lives
but shine through us to the world

༺❀༅❀༅❀༅

Father God,
in a world filled with the sounds of living
it is so easy to ignore Your voice
as You speak through the noise of traffic,
the bustle of the shopping mall,
the jangling of machinery,
the ringing of phones,
our television screens.
We hear the shouted remark
across a crowded street,
acknowledge a friendly wave,
respond to the phone's insistent tone,
follow intently the lives and conversations
of favourite soap stars
yet fail to hear that still small voice - Your voice
that can still be heard above and through the distractions
of our daily lives if we choose to listen.
As always, it's down to choice.
Forgive our selective deafness
our 'haven't got the time' excuses
and help us choose to find time to listen
to the one voice
that really matters.

It is who You are and what You have done
for each one of us that brings us to our knees, Lord.
The only response to such love poured down
and overflowing is to ask for forgiveness.
Forgiveness for being part of a world
that condemned Your Son to death.
Who chose a robber to live in His place
and in doing so robbed the world of its Saviour.
Forgiveness for not always comprehending
that even this was part of Your plan.
That through the blindness of mankind
You would bring us back into the light of Your presence.
Forgiveness for underestimating Your love for me
a sinner.
Father, forgive.

We can never match Your perfection, Lord
Try as we might we stumble and fall
grasping for that which we feel is unobtainable
We are nothing if not consistent
in our falling from Your grace.
For You are perfect love and we most certainly are not.
Perfect love casts out fear
and we are fearful -
fearful of the unknown;
fearful of failure

> *'Son, I never ask for the impossible*
> *I never set a goal that cannot be reached,*
> *a mountain that cannot be climbed*
> *even by those of a nervous disposition.*
> *All I ask is that you come to me as you are*
> *at this moment in time and accept me as I AM.*
> *There is no part of you that cannot be made clean*
> *renewed, restored.*
> *Don't stumble, hold out your hand instead.*
> *That's not too much to ask  -  is it?'*

Loving Father, all the fancy words in the world
expressed in eloquent prose; decorated with emotion
spoken with conviction
cannot compete with a heartfelt 'sorry'
when all other words fail.
There are times when we are all too aware
of our limitations, conscious of sin
and the distance it creates between us.
Sometimes 'sorry' is all the heart can bear to say aloud.
It is only You who can read and understand
the language of our hearts.
Only You who can translate our 'sorry'
into the prayer we would have prayed
if we had the words within us.
Then You forgive - and having forgiven
surround us in an embrace of love
drawing us close to Your heart
as it was always meant to be.
Thank You, Loving Father, that You listen to hearts
as well as voices.  Thank You!

Your forgiveness is total
no notebook, tape recorder or post-it note
to remind You of that moment when.........
You take our confession
offered with hands outstretched
and gently, like the loving heavenly Father that You are
put it to one side to be forgotten.
No grudges, no itching for judgement.
No resentment or ill-will.
Not like us who find it easy to say sorry
but so hard to forgive absolutely.
Forgive us, Father,
that we are often more willing to accept forgiveness
than to forgive.
More willing to accept Your love
than to share it with those who have hurt us.
Teach us to forgive - as You forgive

Love - has its source in You, Creator God.
Flows from You like an ocean
into a world as unyielding as any shoreline cliff.
And like the ocean which batters,
erodes and wears away even the hardest stone
Your love persists -
finds cracks and inlets in hardened hearts
flows inside and works a miracle.
Who would think that water
was more powerful than granite
love mightier than the hardest heart
Thank You, Creator God,
for the power of Your love.

Father, we are so hesitant
in asking for healing
real physical healing.
So hesitant in asking
Your Spirit to touch our lives.
It is almost as if we are afraid
that in hoping for a trickle
we unleash a torrent.
Forgive our timidity, Father,
our lack of faith
in the Creator of this universe.
Forgive our unbelief
as we take Your Word,
apply it to our hearts,
open the floodgates
and anticipate a deluge.

Just a mustard seed, You said.
Just a mustard seed of faith to remove
the mountain of doubts and difficulties
which beset our often frail existence.
We readily confess, Lord Jesus,
that there are times when we reach out
seemingly in vain for that mustard seed.
And yet, if we did but think for a moment,
in that very act of reaching out
we reveal the presence
of the very seed that we seek.
Lord Jesus, we have faith in Your power to heal;
but lack the self-confidence to ask.
We have faith in Your ability to mend broken hearts;
but lack the experience in our own lives.
We have faith in Your power to bring wholeness
into lives that are incomplete;
but hesitate to trouble You with our prayers.
We are like children, Lord Jesus,
standing here in awe of Your power and love -
afraid to ask that which we know is possible -
because we are afraid of the consequences of our asking.
Lord Jesus, accept the mustard seed
that we hold out to You, hearts outstretched.
Take it, and the prayers that we offer,
and grant us the grace to accept
that our prayers are heard, and answered at the moment of asking,
by a God who knows our own incompleteness
and is working to make us whole.

Sometimes, Heavenly Father,
the answer has to be 'I don't know'.
'I don't know why there is so much suffering in the world'.
'I don't know why that child was not restored to full health'.
'I don't know why people can be so cruel, uncaring, selfish'.
Platitudes cannot console a grieving parent,
a starving child, a battered wife.
Sometimes, Heavenly Father, our faith is challenged by this world -

a world that is less concerned with others than with self.
Sometimes, in being honest, we open ourselves to ridicule.
The world would prefer certainty;
but the only certainty is You who created humankind
with the capacity for good and ill
and gave the world Your Son whom we crucified.
'I don't know' might seem a lame excuse to some; uncertainty.
But we trust in Your eternal love for a mankind which has fallen.
We thank You that we are not robots
but have freedom of choice.
Help us to make right choices - choices that affect lives.
Help us to play our part in changing this world
rather than merely sitting back as spectators and criticising.
Help us to see this world through Your eyes of love.

I prayed
"Please Lord,
my life is a mess,
let Your love flow through me
and bring healing".
And like a river
of cool refreshing water
You flowed through me.
Not as a gentle stream
a rivulet of hope
but a torrent
sweeping debris away.
All those broken branches
rust-encrusted items
and accumulated debris
which were holding back the flow
swept aside in a torrent of love
flooding through my veins,
pouring into my heart,
filling my life.
This is healing.
Thank You, Lord!

When I pray for healing Lord, I sometimes feel so inadequate,
ill-equipped for the task.
There are so many I could name who are in need of healing.
There are those who hurt physically
and others whose hurts go deeper
whose scars cannot be seen to the naked eye.
Yet all need healing - all need making whole again.
There are broken bones and broken hearts, Lord.
You had a way - a gentle and loving way
of dealing with hurts; physical and spiritual.
You healed the whole person
something medicine can never do.
You reached the very cause not just the symptoms.
When I pray for healing Lord,
I sometimes feel so inadequate, ill-equipped for the task.
All I can do is bring their names to Your feet
holding them tightly in my prayers,
then hand them over for You to touch
in the way that only You can touch.

꧁ ꧁ ꧁

For those whose lives are broken by distress
**ALL:** **May the God of healing restore you**
For those whose lives are broken by fear
**ALL:** **May the God of healing restore you**
For those whose lives are broken by anger
**ALL:** **May the God of healing restore you**
For those whose lives are broken by pain
**ALL:** **May the God of healing restore you**
For those whose lives are broken by illness
**ALL:** **May the God of healing restore you**
For those whose lives are broken by sin
**ALL:** **May the God of healing restore you**

God of healing, gently touch these lives with Your Spirit.
Bring warmth and comfort, life and wholeness,
restoration into fractured lives and souls.

# The Cross

'A cross is not just a piece of wood.
It is everything that makes life difficult.'
*Leonardo Boff*

'Jesus now has many lovers of His heavenly kingdom,
but few bearers of His cross.'
*Thomas à Kempis*

'The cross that Jesus tells us to carry is the one that we willingly
take up ourselves - the cross of self-denial in order that we might
live for the glory of the Father.'
*Colin Urquhart*

## Stages

From the beginning You knew the final outcome -
watched as the jigsaw pieces were slotted into place -
saw the significance of every moment.
As Your body was anointed with oil at the table of Simon the Leper
the picture was becoming clearer - not only in Your eyes
but to an unknown woman and one of Your closest friends.
Judas sensed that this was his moment;
sacrificing trust that had been so freely given, on the altar of selfish gain,
for his fifteen allotted minutes of fame and thirty pieces of silver.
The woman recognised the moment.
She gave generously, unselfishly, a costly gift, freely offered.
A fragrant sacrifice of perfume and love remembered forever in Your heart.
And as Judas slipped away unnoticed Your disciples saw none of this,
failed to see the significance of the moment.
Two sacrifices, one of trust and one of love.
But You noticed, Lord, as You notice each day
our sacrificial offering and betrayal.

There are people we like and those we do not
but the difficult situations arise when those we love
turn against us for no logical reason.
We are hurt and angry at such betrayal
when someone who has shared our lives
should now use that knowledge against us.
It is a broken relationship, Lord
almost impossible to repair.
That You should share bread and wine at the same table as Judas
knowing the secrets of his heart.
That You could share Your love knowing what was to follow
on the road to Calvary - defies our human understanding.
And yet, Lord, this is the road You would have us follow,
the road that leads to the cross
the road that only makes sense when seen through Your eyes
the road of sacrificial love.

How often when weary do we sigh
'The spirit is willing, but the body is weak.'
How often when in prayer are thoughts distracted
by sounds or circumstance
or prayers diverted by trivial concerns.
Baggage carried with us rather than left at Your feet.
How often do we find ourselves apologising to You
for our abbreviated prayer life.
And yet You draw us still to be in Your presence
as You did the disciples at Gethsemene.
You want us to share in Your life to play our part.
You told Your disciples to watch and pray
so that they might not fall into temptation.
Do You ask the same of us and do we also fail You
each time we whisper
'The spirit is willing, but the body is weak.'?
Grant us the strength Lord, of body and of spirit
to offer You the sacrifice of our lives.

When the going gets tough - the tough get going.
It is easy to say 'No', to take the easy way out.
Easy to play safe and live to fight another day.
Like Peter, who loved You
with such a passion, Lord;
filled with such energy,
so impetuous,
ready to speak first
and ask questions later.
Except when asked
if he was with You, Lord.
Except when his faith was seriously challenged,
when the road to the cross became dangerous.
You knew Peter - knew the calibre of the man
and what would happen before the cock crowed twice.
But it didn't stop You choosing him
the rock upon which Your Church would be built.
There is comfort for us Lord, in Peter's frailty;
reassurance that Your love and confidence extends
to both strong and frail
as You look to our potential
and in Your love forget our momentary weakness.

Twice the cock crowed
and by it the whole world knew
that Peter had denied his Lord.
The echo of that moment
can still be heard today
each time we hide our face
afraid not of death
but a mild rebuke
or at the worst a little ridicule.
The world may never know
our silent denial for as yet, Lord
it has not known
our silent faith.

Lamb of God, You shed for me
Your life upon a blood stained tree,
Your life for mine, love re-defined
An offering, a ransom, release
You gave so much - O Lamb of God

**ALL:** **Just as I am, I come**

The doubts I have, the pain I feel
When at Your feet I humbly kneel
You take it all, both great and small
Give freedom, forgiveness and peace
I have the choice - O Lamb of God

**ALL:** **Just as I am, I come**

Lamb of God, I hear Your voice,
And hearing know I have a choice
To make a start, within my heart
A willingness, to journey by faith
You ask no more - O Lamb of God

**ALL:** **Just as I am, I come**

By waters still, through fire and storm
Your love continues to transform
And with that call, You welcome all
No barriers now, no limits, just grace
No more excuses! - Lamb of God

**ALL:** **Just as I am, I come**

In our walk to the cross and beyond;
who will roll the stone away - show us the empty tomb
- our risen Saviour – Messiah.
Only You, Lord, as You revealed Yourself
to three women early on that Resurrection morning.
Only You, Lord, as You revealed Yourself
to hesitant and frightened disciples in the upper room
and showed Your wounded side.
Only You, Lord, as You revealed Yourself
through the power of Your Holy Spirit
on that Pentecost morning;

and reveal Your self today through tongues of fire
and through the gentlest of breeze
through revelation and revolution in hearts and souls.
In our walk to the cross and beyond
who will roll the stone away - show us the empty tomb
- our risen Saviour - Messiah
Only You, Lord!  Only You!

Worthy are You!
Worthy are You Lamb of God to receive from us
the worship and praise that's due Your name
as with the angels we proclaim:
Worthy are You!
Worthy are You!
Lamb of God, slain for us
You shed Your blood
to pay the price
of sinfulness through sacrifice.
Now to Him who sits on the throne
and the Lamb who leads us home
be Praise and Honour
and Glory and Power
for ever and ever
Amen

# Journeying

'The longest journey is the journey inward.'
*Dag Hammarskjöld*

'In our journey towards God we proceed like those small birds
whose flight is in loops. They always seem to be about to drop,
but the drop in their flight seems to urge them forwards.'
*Gerard W. Hughes*

'In thy journeys to and fro
God direct thee;
In thy happiness and pleasure
God bless thee;
In care, anxiety or trouble
God sustain thee;
In peril and in danger
God protect thee.'
*Timothy Olufosoye*

In my journeying with You
may I never lose my sense of direction,
never lose sight of the landmark
towards which I travel.
And should cloud or rain obscure my vision
may I draw closer to You,
so that my feet may tread
in Your footsteps.
Your words be my encouragement
and Your love my protection
against the storms that assail me.

Your light is the only light I need
as I travel through life's mystery.
Your word the only voice I hear,
that still small voice that leads me
to the place where I should be.
Your presence is the only company I need
as I walk this narrow road.
Your fellowship the warmth I crave
to help me on my way.

In all our travelling:
**ALL: May Your footsteps guide us.**

In our journeying to work and returning:
**ALL: May Your footsteps guide us.**

Within our homes and families:
**ALL: May Your footsteps guide us.**

In our leisure time together:
**ALL: May Your footsteps guide us.**

In difficult situations and conflict:
**ALL: May Your footsteps guide us.**

As we stumble on the way:
**ALL: May Your footsteps guide us.**

In the travelling of our faith:
**ALL: May Your footsteps guide us.**

As we place our trust in You:
**ALL: May Your footsteps guide us.**

In all our travelling, Lord,
may it be Your footsteps
in which we place our feet.

Your life was a journey
from the moment You were born.
From birth to death.
From Bethlehem's stable to Calvary's cross.
How often we fail to understand
that the conclusion of Your journey was inevitable
that You understood this from the very beginning
and yet still walked the path that was Yours to take.
By comparison the many choices we make
in our life seem trivial.
The twists and turns we choose
are often taken on impulse
with no clear comprehension of the outcome.
Thank You, Jesus.
Thank You that You loved humankind enough
to make that journey
even as You felt the pain of rejection;
the pain of the lashes,
the pain of the nails,
the pain of the cross.

Our walk with God is never a lonely walk.
It is a family occasion
if taken in the company of God's children.
If we lag behind there are those who will turn
and offer words of encouragement,
hold out a hand and offer assistance
over stiles and other obstacles, share refreshment,
help us from our knees when we stumble.
Our walk with God is never a lonely walk.
It is a joyful experience as along the path others join us
attracted by the company of God's children
singing the same songs of praise that angels sing
following a path worn down by tears and joy
and sacrifice.
Our walk with God is never a lonely walk
for He walks with us on a track that leads
to a glorious destination.

How big is your God?
Can He destroy whole armies,
bring nations to their knees,
cause the heavens to roar,
the lightning to flash,
the sun to shine,
the rain to fall?
Can He pour out His love
upon a single child,
bind a broken heart,
be a still small voice,
a comforter of all?
Can He love so much
as to suffer the pain
of rejection, betrayal,
death on a cross
for the sake of those
who never knew Him at all?
Can He rise again
to show the power of a love
even death can't defeat,
love that draws mankind
once more
into fellowship
with him?
How big is your God?

# Opening/Closing Worship

Here we are Lord; Your people,
Your Church - meeting together in Your presence.
We welcome each other and we welcome You.
Make Yourself known to us in new ways
through our worship, our prayers
and our understanding of Your Word today.

Through our hymns and songs,
our prayer and meditation,
the joining of our lives in fellowship
we worship You,
Father Son and Holy Spirit.
Enfold us in Your love,
and empower our worship
that Your name might be glorified in this place
and in our lives.

We are gathered here today, Lord God
as Your people to offer You
our sacrifice of prayer and worship.
We come from different walks of life;
some are well educated, others not;
some have walked with You for many years,
others are just starting their journey;
some are strong, others weak;
some are full of joy, others burdened by care.
You love each of us in equal measure.
You pour Your blessings on us in equal measure.

We have gathered here today, Lord God
as Your people to offer You
our sacrifice of prayer and worship.
We have fed on Your Word,
been refreshed through Your living water,
felt the encircling of Your Spirit
around this fellowship and around individual lives.
As we go from this place
may we continue to know Your presence and power
in the very different lives that we lead,
to Your praise and glory.

As we take our worship, praise and prayer
from this place and into our daily lives,
may our lives be sustained
through the love of our Heavenly Father.
May we feel the presence of our Saviour
walking beside us,
and know the power of the Spirit
in both our actions and our words.

# A Little Litany and Liturgy

The Oxford Dictionary of the Christian Church describes litany as:

*'A form of prayer consisting of a series of petitions or biddings sung or said by a deacon, priest, or cantors, to which the people make a fixed response. The litany apparently originated at Antioch in the 4th century, spreading to Constantinople and later to the West. Pope Gelasius I (492-6) introduced into the Mass a litanic intercession, of which the Kyrie (the response prayer Kyrie Eleison - Lord, have mercy) is the sole surviving relic.'*

To illustrate the way in which the Jews used what we now call a litany, we have only to look at the 136th Psalm which was used in the public worship of the Temple, being recited alternately by priest and people.

> [1] Oh, give thanks to the LORD, for He is good!
> **For His mercy *endures* forever.**
> [2] Oh, give thanks to the God of gods!
> **For His mercy *endures* forever.**
> [3] Oh, give thanks to the Lord of lords!
> **For His mercy *endures* forever:**
> [4] To Him who alone does great wonders,
> **For His mercy *endures* forever;**
> [5] To Him who by wisdom made the heavens,
> **For His mercy *endures* forever...**
> [6] To Him who laid out the earth above the waters,
> **For His mercy *endures* forever;**
> [7] To Him who made great lights,
> **For His mercy *endures* forever—**
> [8] The sun to rule by day,
> **For His mercy *endures* forever;**
> [9] The moon and stars to rule by night,
> **For His mercy *endures* forever.**
> [10] To Him who struck Egypt in their firstborn,
> **For His mercy *endures* forever;**
> [11] And brought out Israel from among them,
> **For His mercy *endures* forever;**
> [12] With a strong hand, and with an outstretched arm,
> **For His mercy *endures* forever;**

[13] To Him who divided the Red Sea in two,
**For His mercy *endures* forever;**
[14] And made Israel pass through the midst of it,
**For His mercy *endures* forever;**
[15] But overthrew Pharaoh and his army in the Red Sea,
**For His mercy *endures* forever;**
[16] To Him who led His people through the wilderness,
**For His mercy *endures* forever;**

*(Psalm 136 in NKJ version)*

In like manner we find in the Book of Daniel the canticle of the three youths in the fiery furnace; each verse ends with the words, "Praise and exalt Him above all for ever".

## What is liturgy?

Again, according from the Oxford Dictionary of the Christian Church the word is used in two senses;

Firstly it relates to all of the prescribed services of the Church, as contrasted with private devotions.
Secondly and especially in the Eastern Church it describes the Eucharist.

In practice, liturgy is a set of responsive prayers that enable a congregation to participate in the dialogue of worship. In some traditions congregational participation is the norm and done freely and openly through words, song and action.

To others it is not, and a liturgy enables a person to feel a part of the worship and prayer offering to God, in a way that they might not if it were all led from the front.

## Father

It's that picture of God the Father as potter… 'Yet, O Lord, You are our Father. We are the clay, You are the potter; we are the work of Your hand.'

**All: May we, through Your creative power demonstrate our true potential**

It's that picture of a father welcoming home the prodigal son, arms open wide ready to accept, embrace and enfold.

63

**All: May we know the warmth and abiding love of Your embrace**

It's that picture of Jesus standing in the river, as God announces to the universe that 'This is my Son, whom I love; with Him I am well pleased'

**All: May we understand our own worth, and that of our neighbour in Your eyes**

It's that picture of Jesus walking to a lonely place to be quiet and be at one with His Heavenly Father

**All: May we find place in our lives to be quiet, to be close to You**

It's that picture of God's own Son in the Garden of Gethsemene showing perfect obedience: 'Yet not as I will, but as You will'

**All: Grant us the strength to be obedient to Your will, even when it hurts**

## <u>Son</u>

Lord Jesus, Son of God, Saviour of the world

**All: Be the centre of all that we are, and the life that we lead**

Lord Jesus, Light in this dark World, illuminate our hearts and minds.

**All: Be the centre of all that we are, and the life that we lead**

Lord Jesus, Bread of Life, feed us in those times of emptiness and hunger

**All: Be the centre of all that we are, and the life that we lead**

Lord Jesus, Water of Life, flow through our hearts and into our lives

**All: Be the centre of all that we are, and the life that we lead**

Lord Jesus, may ours be fruitful lives as branches and shoots of the one True Vine

**All: Be the centre of all that we are, and the life that we lead**

Lord Jesus, Servant King may we understand the true meaning of service

**All: Be the centre of all that we are, and the life that we lead**

Lord Jesus, for whom death could claim no victory, may we live in the knowledge and assurance of Your Resurrection

# Spirit

Holy Spirit, giver of life, creative breath of God through whom this world was breathed into existence and is sustained

**All:  Blow through the parched earth of our existence, and breathe Your Life into our lives.**

Spirit of Truth and Wisdom through ages past and present who guides God's people into all Truth

**All:  Blow through the parched earth of our knowledge, and breathe Your Truth into our lives.**

Holy Spirit, Counsellor, sent by the Father; convicting, comforting, guiding and reassuring

**All:  Blow through the parched earth of our faith, and breathe peace, love and reassurance into our lives.**

Holy Spirit, enabler of Your servants and prophets through the ages. Source of authority, wisdom and power

**All:  Blow through the parched earth of our lives and breathe into them Your Spirit's power**

Holy Spirit, indwelling presence of God, empowering the lives of the apostles at Pentecost and the Church today

**All:  Blow through the parched earth of our witness, and empower our lives in the service of Your Kingdom**

# Wholeness

Jesus, You came that we might have life, and have it abundantly

**ALL: Precious Jesus, we offer You our praise and thanks.**

You poured living water into lives that were parched and thirsty

**ALL: Precious Jesus, we offer You our praise and thanks.**

You fed souls that were hungry with the bread of life

**ALL: Precious Jesus, we offer You our praise and thanks.**

You brought healing through a touch that knew no prejudice or barrier

**ALL: Precious Jesus, we offer You our praise and thanks.**

You brought Salvation through the cross,

**ALL: Precious Jesus, we offer You our praise and thanks.**

You brought a means through which mankind could be made right again with its Creator

**ALL: Precious Jesus, we offer You our praise and thanks.**

You brought comfort to the sorrowing, liberty to the poor

**ALL: Precious Jesus, we offer You our praise and thanks.**

You accept us as we are, and mould us into the people we were meant to be

**ALL: Precious Jesus, we offer You our praise and thanks.**

You enable broken lives and relationships to be made whole again

**ALL: Precious Jesus, we offer You our praise and thanks**

I will extol the Lord at all times:

**ALL: His praise will always be on my lips.**

I sought the Lord and He answered me; He delivered me from all my fears:

**ALL: His praise will always be on my lips.**

Those who look to Him are radiant; their faces are never covered with shame:

**ALL: His praise will always be on my lips.**

Taste and see that the Lord is good; blessed is the man who takes refuge in him:

**ALL: His praise will always be on my lips.**

Fear the Lord, You His saints, for those who fear Him lack nothing

**ALL: His praise will always be on my lips**

The lions may grow weak and hungry, but those who seek the Lord lack no good thing:

**ALL: His praise will always be on my lips.**

The eyes of the Lord are on the righteous, and His ears attentive to their cry

**ALL: His praise will always be on my lips**

The righteous cry out, and the Lord hears them; He delivers them from all their troubles:

**ALL: His praise will always be on my lips.**

The Lord is close to the broken hearted, and saves those who are crushed in spirit:

**ALL: His praise will always be on my lips.**

Yes, I will extol the Lord at all times:

**ALL: His praise will always be on my lips.**

*(Psalm 34)*

Father God, in whose love we live and move, we pray for a world crying out to feel loved, wanted, cherished and unique.

**ALL: Heavenly Father, source of all love.**

We pray for a world torn apart by conflict and war.
A world that lives uneasily in a climate of fear
with no clear vision for future days.

**ALL: Heavenly Father, source of all hope.**

We pray for a world that thinks less of others than of self.
A world where division between nations, race, religion
neighbour and family leads to distrust.

**ALL: Heavenly Father, source of all peace.**

We pray for a world that is short on happiness,
too busy to enjoy this world You have created,
too preoccupied with living to appreciate life.

**ALL: Heavenly Father, source of all joy.**

We pray for a world where spiritual longing is satisfied
by fashionable notions and temporary solutions
with no thought for tomorrow.

**ALL: Heavenly Father, source of our Salvation.**

We pray for a world that needs to know Your love, Your hope,
Your peace, Your joy and Salvation. A world that needs to know
it is special, unique and is uniquely loved by a Heavenly Father.

# People

We're here again, Lord,
Your family, in fellowship together.
Friends, strangers, colleagues, neighbours.
Short, tall, rich and poor.
An assortment of Your people with one purpose and one aim;
to learn from You and to worship You.
Be with us in our diversity.
Join us in unity through Your love
that we might leave this place
knowing that we have met not only with each other
but also with You!

All: **In the midst of darkness,**
**this world, this country, this city, this street,**
**this place in which we meet,**
**it is Your light by which we see.**
**All others too dim to break through the smog**
**that conceals Your glory to our neighbour.**
**May Your light so shine in our lives**
**that others might see You**
**and seeing You respond -**
**hold out their hand to grasp the flame**
**that cuts through the grime of lives spoiled and cloudy**
**to show the beauty of the person within.**

*Psalm 85*

I am listening to what the Lord God is saying;
He promises peace to us, His own people,
if we do not go back to our foolish ways.
Surely He is ready to save those who honour Him
and His saving presence will remain in our land

All: **Love and faithfulness will meet; righteousness and peace will**
**embrace. Man's loyalty will reach up from the earth, and God's**
**righteousness will look down from heaven.**

God of city, town and village, we see You both in the spectacular and in
the ordinariness of life. In the beauty of a sunset behind a city skyline and
in the selfless giving of time to ones in need; in the tranquillity of the
dawn chorus and the roar of a jet engine.

Open our eyes:

**All:** **That we might see.**
Our skills, our knowledge, our wisdom
all have their origins with You.
Open our minds:

**All:** **That we might understand.**
Our creativity, our art, our poetry, our visual expressions are
reflections of Your creativity, Your Spirit working in us and
around us.
Open our imaginations:

**All:** **That we might explore our own creativity.**

God of all, we were not all born to be rich or famous, but we were all born
with the potential to become the people whom You would have us be.

**All: Help us to see the potential within the lives of others - especially**
**those we would not naturally choose as friends or neighbours.**
**Help us to become the people You would have us be.**
**Help us realise our true potential.**

May the God of diversity draw us close to each other here today;
old and young, weak and strong, wise and simple.
Together we are the body of Christ in this place.
Together we are strong, bound together by the bonds of Your love.
Together we can explore together the wonder that is mankind; our own
uniqueness, our own self-worth.
May the Holy Spirit grant us the wisdom to see the potential in ourself
and others; the knowledge to understand that all mankind has its origins
in the Godhead and the understanding that His love extends to all that He
has created.

# Family

'I rejoiced with those who said to me, "Let us go to the house of the Lord."'

**All: 'How good it is to sing praises to our God, how pleasant and fitting to praise him!'**

As Your family we gather here today.
Not because we have to, but because we want to.
We are here to offer You our worship, our prayers
and our lives in service to You and to our neighbour.
We have as our example Your Son who chose not to rule but to serve,
who gave of himself and You a love so strong that it flowed like a river
from His hands and His heart.

Your Son, who came that we might have life, and have it abundantly:

**All: Thanks be to God.**

Your Son, who came that we might know love, and knowing, might share:

**All: Thanks be to God.**

Your Son, who emptied himself of life and love, that we might be filled with both:

**All: Thanks be to God.**

'How great is the love the Father has lavished upon us':

**ALL: That we should be called children of God'**

*1 John 3:1*

Father, we come here today conscious of our shortcomings, aware of the thoughts, actions and deeds which have not reflected Your love:

**All: Jesus, Lord of Love have mercy on us.**

Father, our lives are filled with comings and goings,
so little time to be still, so little time for others,
for giving instead of receiving:

**All: Jesus, Lord of Life have mercy on us.**

Father, in a world that needs to know Your love
forgive us those times when impatience, tiredness, selfishness or
insensitivity have made it difficult for others to see Your love through our
lives:

**All: Jesus, Servant of all have mercy on us.**

In a moment of silence we bring to our Heavenly Father the needs of our friends and families; the tensions, the harsh words spoken in haste, the good deed not done, the love not shown.

*(Silence)*

We also remember the needs of the Church family, both here and world-wide.

*(Silence)*

**All: God of family, God of Love, forgive us for those times when we have forgotten how much we are loved by You, and how important a part we play in Your family. Forgive us when we take family for granted.**

You are merciful, Lord! You are kind and patient and always loving.
You are good to everyone, and You take care of all Your creation.
All creation will thank You, and Your loyal people will praise You.

*Psalm 145*

Together we say the words of The Lord's Prayer:

**All: Our Father......**

Blessed be God, Father, Son and Holy Spirit. Glorious Trinity

**All: Blessed be our God for ever.**

May we know the love of the heavenly Father deep in our hearts.
May we understand our significance in the centre of His family, and the bonds that hold us so close as brother and sister.
May we understand the lengths that He was prepared to go for all mankind and freely respond in the Today which He has given for us to cherish.

**All: Amen**

# Creation

God of storm and rain cloud, of wind and biting cold,
of hail, thunder and flood.
In darker days, loud and fearful days
we see something of Your awesome power
and recognise our own weakness;
our own inability to control the elements.
God of sunshine and birdsong, of calm mists and warm breezes,
slow moving streams, and blossoming trees.
In lighter days, fun-filled brighter days
we see something of Your overwhelming love
and recognise our own unworthiness.
Help us to recognise You within the elements of Your created world
and be grateful!

You have set Your glory above the heavens. From the lips of children and infants You have ordained praise:

**All: O Lord, our Lord, how majestic is Your name in all the earth.**

When I consider Your heavens, the work of Your fingers, the moon and the stars which You have set in place, what is man that You are mindful of him, the son of man that You are for him:

**All: O Lord, our Lord, how majestic is Your name in all the earth.**

You made him a little lower than the heavenly beings and crowned him with glory and honour. You made him ruler over the works of Your hands; You put everything under His feet.

**All: O Lord, our Lord, how majestic is Your name in all the earth.**

You alone are the Lord; You have made heaven,
The heaven of heavens, with all their host,                    *Neh 9:6*

Exposed by the brightness of Your Glory, the exuberance of Your creative Spirit, our lives can look so barren, so shallow Creator God:

**All: Create a right spirit within us.**

Exposed by the inclusiveness of Your love, for Your willingness to give Your own Son not just for one people but for all mankind Loving God:

**All: Teach us how to Love.**

Exposed by the humility of Your Son, who came to earth as Servant King, washing feet rather than waging war - God of all:

All: **Help us to serve.**

Creator God, Loving God, God of all, we stand here today exposed and vulnerable:

All: **Forgive us when we fall short of Your expectations. Forgive us for our lack of love. Forgive us those times when through pride we fail to serve others as You did. Forgive us when we forget who we are, and whom we serve.**

'Christ was chosen even before the world was created, but because of you, He did not come until these last days. And when He did come, it was to lead you to have faith in God, who raised Him from death and honored Him in a glorious way. That's why you have put your faith and hope in God.'                                   *1 Peter 1: 20, 21*

Let us join together in the words of the Lord 's prayer:

**ALL: Our Father...**

All: **Creator God, You are worthy of our praise and worship.**
**Make us worthy of the world in which You have placed us.**
**Help us to accept the value You place on each one of us.**
**Empower us in our stewardship of Your garden and in the daily task of spreading the Good News of Your creative and redeeming Love.**
**Make us one in purpose, as You are one with Jesus and the Holy Spirit.**

                                                            **Amen**

# Raised with Christ

'Since, then, You have been raised with Christ, set Your hearts on things above, where Christ is seated at the right hand of God.'      *Col 3:1*

**All: Father God, be with us in our worship, in our prayers and in our reading of Your word. Be with us in our fellowship one with another. Be with us in our agreement and disagreement. Be with us in our unity and diversity. Be with us as we grow together, born again and joined together into Your heavenly family.**

For God so loved the world:

**All: That He gave His one and only Son**

That whoever believes in Him shall not perish

**All: But have eternal life.**

'Set your minds on things above, and not on earthly things. For you died, and your life is now hidden with Christ in God. When Christ, who is your life, appears, then you will also appear with Him in glory.'      *Col 3:3*

For those times when our eyes have been short-sighted, when we have failed to see Your vision for our lives:

**All: Help us focus on You.**

For those times when we choose not to give but to store up treasures for our own use. When we lose sight of our own worth.

**All: Help us focus on You.**

For those times when Your sacrificial love has meant less than it should

**All: Help us focus on You.**

For those times when our feet have stayed firmly in this world, rather than walking in Your footsteps

**All: Help us focus on You.**

For all those times when we have failed to acknowledge in our own hearts that we are a new creation, raised to life with Christ

**All: Father, forgive.**

'Therefore, as God's chosen people, holy and dearly loved, clothe Yourself with compassion, kindness, humility, gentleness and patience. Bear with each other and forgive whatever grievances You may have against one another.

Forgive as the Lord forgave You. And above all this put on love

**All: Which binds all these in perfect unity.'**

Let us share a time of quiet reflection, bringing to the feet of our God the prayers of our hearts and the remembrance of our own awakening to spiritual life with Christ.

*(Silence)*

Let's share in the pattern of prayer that Jesus taught His disciples...

**All: Our Father.....**

O Lord open our lips:

**All: And our mouths will declare Your praise.**

O Lord You do not delight in sacrifice, or I would bring it; You do not delight in burnt offerings:

**All: The sacrifices of God are a humble spirit. He will not reject a humble and repentant heart.**

Gracious and loving Father, in accepting Your call on our lives, we left self behind and took on the new mantle of Your sacrificial love.

**All: Together we share in Your sacrifice and the resurrection life of Jesus.**

In doing so we acknowledged Your supreme act of love in giving Your Son to this world, and also our share of mankind's guilt in the cross.

**All: Together we share in Your sacrifice and the resurrection life of Jesus.**

We looked from the sorrow of Good Friday to the joy of Easter and the promise of the Resurrection. We now share together in that promise and look forward with anticipation to spending an eternity in Your presence. God of sacrifice and love

**All: Together we share in Your sacrifice and the resurrection life of Jesus.**

# A God of Expression

God smiles, this much I know; for He created laughter - so that we might join in the enjoyment of His creative energy; those wonderful colour schemes of bird butterfly and flower, the shapes and expressions on so many creatures and insects.

These weren't created by a boring God - they were drawn and planned by a God with a sense of humour - and that's a comforting thought!

Creator God, we praise You for the diversity of Your world and for the life You have breathed into all things.

**ALL: For the colours we see**

The sounds we hear

**ALL: The textures we feel**

For the large

**ALL: And the small**

The fierce

**ALL: And the timid**

Predator

**ALL: And prey**

Creator God, we thank You for Your creation, perfect in its design and purpose, perfect in its diversity and unity.

Psalm 19
How clearly the sky reveals God's glory!

**All: How plainly it shows what He has done!**

Each day announces it to the following day.

**All: Each night repeats it to the next.**

No speech or words are used, no sound is heard

**All: Yet their message goes out to all the world and is heard to the ends
of the earth.**

Creator God, Your Spirit enables our own creative abilities as we allow Him to work through our words, our hands and our imaginations.
We thank You for the beauty of created things, for pots and bowls moulded by the skilful manipulation of clay, for a portrait which captures the essence of a personality, for the written word which transports us to a

faraway place, a poem that captures the raw emotion of a moment, a prayer that speaks to our heart and soul.

You are present wherever mankind opens its eyes to see, can be heard whenever mankind opens its ears to hear, can be felt as hands are outstretched in faith.

**All: As the wind blows across this land where it wills, so Your loving Spirit blows in us and through us.**
**As the sun warms the cold earth after the chill of night, so Your love warms our hearts with joy.**
**And Your touch brings a peace into our restless lives.**

God of Love, God of Joy and God of Peace, may we know all three as we open our eyes to the wonders of this garden in which You have placed us and begin to recognise the image of Your love within the selfless actions of others.

Creator God, we pray for Your Kingdom, established here on earth wherever You reign in hearts open to the expression of Your praise and glory.

**All: Your Kingdom Come**

But we also look forward an eternity in Your Kingdom, Your promise to all who truly believe

**All: On earth as it is in heaven**

We take a moment of quiet to reflect on the creativity of our God, expressed through the world and through the creativity within each one of us

*(Silence)*

And together we join in the prayer that Jesus taught His disciples.

**All: Our Father……**

God of expression, enable us Your creation to enjoy along with You the sheer exuberance of Your creativity.

**All: Amen.**

# Chosen

'You are a chosen people, a royal priesthood, a holy nation, a people belonging to God, that you might declare the praises of Him who called you out of darkness into His wonderful light'

**All: We declare Your glory to the world, gracious loving Father. We no longer walk in the uncertainty of the darkness but in the certainty of Your glorious light.**

Father God, into Your presence we draw
Your creation worshipping its creator
Your children drawn to the arms of a loving Father.
Thank You that You accept us as we are;
vulnerable, flawed and in need of love
and feed us through word, hymn, song and prayer.
Fill us with the certainty of Your love,
the power of Your Spirit and the joy of Your Kingdom
as we open ourselves in worship,
in service to each other - and to You.

For the responsibilities that are ours, Your ambassadors
as children of light in this dark world:

**All: Enfold us with the brightness of Your Spirit.**

For our timidity and weakness, the lack of faith
which often prevents us from bearing fruit:

**All: Enfold us with the confidence of Your Spirit**

For those times when we feel far away from Your presence
and choose to wander from Your path:

**All: Enfold us with the encouragement of Your Spirit**

For those times when the inner tensions within our lives bring unease and fear:

**All: Enfold us with the serenity of Your Spirit**

'You did not choose me, but I chose you and appointed you
to go and bear fruit - fruit that will last.'

For those times when we forget that we are a chosen people, special, loved and important to Your Kingdom

**All: Enfold us with the truth of Your Spirit**

With all of our strengths and weaknesses, successes and failures we come to Your feet, humbly admitting our faults and trusting You for Your forgiveness.

Fill us

**All: Renew us**

Take us

**All: Use us**

As Your lights in this world of darkness, empowered through Your Spirit

**All: Your Spirit of love**

Your Spirit of peace

**All: Your Spirit of hope**

For a world that lives but has yet to experience life in all its fullness.
For a world that loves, but has yet to meet with the source of all love.
For a world that forever seeks, but stumbles in its searching.

"The unfolding of Your words gives light; it gives understanding to the simple… direct my footsteps according to Your word, let no sin rule over me."                                                                          *Psalm 119*

Let's spend a moment or two in quiet reflection on those words.

*(Silence)*

We join together in the Lord's prayer.

**All: Our Father…**

For Your word which strengthens our faith and empowers our daily lives:

**All: We thank You, Father**

For Your word which speaks to us, teaches, admonishes and encourages:

**All: We thank You, Father**

For Your word which convinces us of our worth and our uniqueness:

**All: We thank You, Father**

For Your word which enables us to share Your love to this dark world:

**All: We thank You, Father**

# Sacrifice

'For I desire mercy, not sacrifice, and acknowledgement of God rather than burnt offerings.'
(Hosea 6:6)

Into Your presence we come, Father God as Your children have done throughout the centuries. In vast Cathedrals, Parish Churches, Chapels, homes, warehouses, converted cinemas, in lonely isolated places. Alone or gathered together with others, Your Church is wherever Your people meet together in worship, in fellowship and in prayer.

Your presence is discernible wherever Your Spirit is allowed to enter:

**All: Be with us now, loving Father**

Into Your presence we come, Father God, mindful of our own failings; our thoughts, words and actions that have shown nothing of Your love

**All: Forgive us, loving Father**

Into Your presence we come, Father God; remembering the sacrifice of Your Son on a cruel cross so that we might know freedom from the guilt of sin, and be made right again with our Creator.

**All: Thank You, loving Father**

'Because he loves me,' says the Lord, 'I will rescue him; I will protect him, for he acknowledges my name.

**All: He will call upon me, and I will answer him; I will be with him in trouble, I will deliver him and honour him.'** *(Psalm 91)*

Thank You, loving Father that You are with us in our joys and our sorrows, the peaks and troughs of our lives, because You understand our human nature. You know our hearts, feel our pain, know our anguish and enfold us with Your love that we might know daily Your forgiveness and healing.

We say together the words of the Lord's Prayer.

**All: Our Father...**

'He is the atoning sacrifice for our sins, and not only for ours but for the sins of the whole world.' *(1 John 2:2)*

For Your love which breathed this world into being, and daily sustains it

**All: We give You thanks**

For Your love which granted mankind free will and choice:

**All: We give You thanks**

For Your love which never fails as we do, but stretches to eternity:

**All: We give You thanks**

For Your love, sacrificed upon a cross for our sake:

**All: We give You thanks**

For Your love which rose triumphant from the grave and lives within us:

**All: We give You thanks**

For Your love which encircles us as we meet together in Your presence:

**All: We give You thanks**

For Your love which extends to all mankind:

**All: We give You thanks**


We spend a moment or two in quiet meditation, thinking of the sacrifice of Jesus; pure Love freely given and poured out for our Salvation.

*(Silence)*

And for the challenge of the sacrificial life that Jesus calls us to live.

*(Silence)*


In a world of self-seeking, of self-sufficiency
there is often very little space for love.
Little time for giving, or receiving.
In the midst of living, the bustle of the shopping centre,
the noise of office or workspace, the party's small-talk;
there is real loneliness - unnoticed by all but You.
Give us discernment, Father to see people as You see them
to be Your love in this world,
to be willing to give sacrificially of time, and self
that others might know the depth of Your love.

**All: In our busy lives, Lord help us to be Your love in the world**


All these things we ask through Your glorious name, loving heavenly Father.

# Revelation

' I want you to know brothers that the Gospel I preached is not something that man made up, I did not receive it from any man, nor was I taught it; rather, I received it by revelation from Jesus Christ.'     *(Gal 1:11)*

Into Your presence we come
Father Son and Holy Spirit , Glorious Trinity.
We are here to listen to Your word as it is revealed to us
and then to act upon it in our daily lives.
We are here to be filled with Your Spirit
and dedicate again our lives to You.
We are here because You call us to service
as You have called Your saints throughout history.
We are here of our own free will.

'This we proclaim concerning the Word of Life.  The life appeared; we have seen it and testify to it, and we proclaim to you the eternal life, which was with the Father and has appeared to us.'     *(1 John 1)*

For the steadfast message of Your prophets through the ages:

**All: Word of life, we thank You**

For the hope and encouragement we find within the Scriptures:

**All: Word of life, we thank You**

For Your Word that comes alive in our hearts as we hear it:

**All: Word of life, we thank You**

For those quiet times alone in Your presence, when You speak directly to our hearts:

**All: Word of life, we thank You**

For the continuing revelation of Your active love for all mankind:

**All: Word of life, we thank You**

'For the word of God *is* living and powerful, and sharper than any two-edged sword, piercing even to the division of soul and spirit, and of joints and marrow, and is a discerner of the thoughts and intents of the heart.'
*Heb 4:12*

We are here today to meet with You, to listen to You.
Through these past days we have listened too much to the noise of this world and not found time to hear Your voice.

**All: Word of life, forgive us**

Through these past days we have made choices without reference to You preferring our own wisdom to Yours.

**All: Word of life, forgive us**

'O Lord You have searched me and You know me. You know when I sit and when I rise; You perceive my thoughts from afar.'

**All: You discern my going out and my lying down; You are familiar with all my ways. Before a word is on my tongue You know it completely, O Lord.'** *(Psalm 139)*

You know us so well, heavenly Father. You gave us the free will to make our own choices, but hold Your arms wide to comfort and forgive us when we fail You, as so often we do.

Such love is beyond our understanding:

**All: Thank You, heavenly Father**

Through our words of prayer and adoration:

**All: We lift Your name on high**

Through our songs of praise and thanksgiving:

**All: We lift Your name on high**

Through our lives, our attitudes and acts of service:

**All: We lift Your name on high**

Together we share in the words of the Lord's prayer

**All: Our Father...**

Word of life, through whom this world was created and all things breathed into existence, may we draw close to You, hear You speaking, understand, and in understanding grow in faith and in service to You and to others.

# Testimony

"I will tell of the kindnesses of the Lord, the deeds for which He is to be praised, according to all the Lord has done for us." *(Isaiah 63)*

Loving Father, we stand here today as testimony to all that You are and all that You mean to us. We stand here today as witnesses in this place to the grace, mercy and love shown to each one of us.
We stand here today as children of a heavenly Father, accepted and loved.

We worship You:

**All: We lift our hearts to You in praise**

We adore You:

**All: We lift our hands to You in praise**

We proclaim Your name:

**All: Within these walls and in our lives, day by day.**

Standing in God's house, in His presence, with His people and sharing in worship together reminds us of that necessary act of confession

Sometimes, Lord it's difficult to find the words of repentance.
Not all of us are poets well versed in public speaking.
Not all of us are confident when conversing with Higher Authorities.
Sometimes, Lord the longest prayer we can utter is a single word.
Not very eloquent.
No Booker prize winner but full of emotion and full of meaning.
Sometimes, Lord all we can say is 'Sorry'.

**ALL: Our God is a loving God, and forgives those who come to Him in humility.**

Thank You Father that You hear the cry of our hearts and not only forgive but forget. Thank You Father for a love that is beyond our understanding.

I will extol the Lord at all times:

**All: His praise will be always on my lips**

Glorify the Lord with me:

**All: Let us exalt His name together**

I sought the Lord and He answered me:

**All: He delivered me from all my fears**

Taste and see that the Lord is good:

**All: Blessed is the man who takes refuge in him.**          *(Psalm 34)*

Father God, when we consider our lives and the compare them to the
depth of Your love shown to the whole of mankind, we stand in awe.
We have this Good News to proclaim;
not just within the walls of this building but in the world outside.
Good News of God's saving grace; Good News of release from fear.
Good News of forgiveness from sin; Good News of wholeness of life.
Good News of eternal life for all who truly believe.

At that time you will say,
"Our LORD, we are thankful, and we worship only You.
We will tell the nations how glorious You are and what You have done.
Because of Your wonderful deeds we will sing Your praises everywhere
on earth."                                              *Is 12:4,5*

This is our testimony

**All: That God's saving grace is for all mankind**

Let's join together in the words of the Lord's prayer

**All: Our Father**

We thank You that through the sacrificial offering of Your Son, Jesus
Christ You have drawn us back into Your family; sons and daughters
together of one heavenly Father.

**All: Through Your Holy Spirit empower us to share this Good News
with others.**

# Worship

'Oh come, let us worship and bow down; Let us kneel before the Lord our
Maker. For He is our God, And we are the people of His pasture,
And the sheep of His hand. '
*(Psalm 95)*

**All: You are worthy, our Lord and God, to receive glory and honour and
power, for You created all things, and by Your will they were
created and have their being.**

You are worthy indeed Lord to receive not just the worship and praise
of our lips, but also of our hearts and souls.
You created all things for a purpose, and we are part of Your purpose
in this place and at this moment in time.

**All: Praise and glory and wisdom and thanks, honour and power and
strength be to our God for ever and ever. Amen**

As we draw close to You, Lord, and the brightness of Your love
we are made only too aware of our own shortcomings.
You planted a garden and set us within to tend and care for it,
created minds to appreciate and voices to raise in worship.

**All: Forgive our neglect of Your garden. Increase our awareness of the
beauty of Your creation and our willingness to praise its creator.**

Through Your Son Jesus Christ You opened up the way
for all to know and worship You.

**All: Forgive us for those times when we ignored opportunities to share
the Good News of Your Love and Grace with others.**

Through the indwelling of Your Spirit You empower Your Church.

**All: Forgive our uncertainty and lack of faith that often causes us to
limit Your power in this present age.**

As we draw close to You in worship, Lord, we trust in Your unfailing
love;
Your forgiving love; Your restoring love.

"For the Lord is a great God, the great King above all gods.
In His hands are the depths of the earth, and the mountain peaks belong
to him.
The sea is his, for He made it, and His hands formed the dry land."
*(Psalm 95)*

In the beauty of this moment
**All: We worship You**
In the fellowship of Your people
**All: We worship You**
In the presence of Your Spirit
**All: We worship You**
In the company of all creation
**All: We worship You**
Father, Son, Holy Spirit, Glorious Trinity
**All: We worship You**

Enfold us in Your love
The warmth of Your love
The comfort of Your love
The reassurance of Your love
The healing of Your love
Enfold us in Your love
**All: That we might share that same love through our lives**

Let us have a time of quiet. A precious moment or two to think about the God we serve, the God we worship, the God we love
*(Silence)*
Let us think about Jesus. His life, His mission, His death and Resurrection
*(Silence)*
Let us think about the Holy Spirit. His power, wisdom and presence in our lives
*(Silence)*

As part of our act of worship we use those words which Jesus himself taught his disciples to pray
**All: Our Father...**

Father God, we join with the Psalmist in declaring 'O Lord God Almighty, who is like You? You are mighty, O Lord, and Your faithfulness surrounds You.'

# Spirit

'And afterward, I will pour out my Spirit on all people. Your sons and daughters will prophesy, your old men will dream dreams, your young men will see visions.'

*(Zec 12:10)*

'Because you are sons, God sent the Spirit of His Son into our hearts, the Spirit who calls out, "Abba, Father."'

*(Gal 4:6)*

Into Your presence we come. Into fellowship with Father, Son and Holy Spirit; Glorious Trinity.

You breathed this world into being. Your creative Spirit is still visible within our everyday lives; through the changing seasons, the colours and sounds of nature, the rhythm of day and night, sunrise and sunset, tide and wind, rain and shine.

**All: Breathe upon our fellowship, Creating Spirit, Creator God**

Your Spirit, present in the birth pangs of this world empowered the Prophets of old, ordinary people called to live extraordinary lives.

**All: Breathe upon our fellowship, Creating Spirit, Creator God**

Your Spirit was so visible through the life of Your Son, from the moment of conception to His death and glorious resurrection.

**All: Breathe upon our fellowship, Creating Spirit, Creator God**

Your Spirit was the parting gift of Jesus to the world. ' You will receive power when the Holy Spirit comes upon You, and You will be my witnesses ... to the ends of the earth.'

**All: Breathe upon our fellowship, Creating Spirit, Creator God**

Father, You have gifted us with the power to perform miracles,
to be Your witnesses here and to the ends of the earth.
Yet we stand so often with feelings of inadequacy
fearful of our own failings and sin.
Forgive us when we try and limit Your power
and underestimate our own capabilities.
Forgive us when we fail to open our hearts fully
to the working of Your Spirit
when we choose to limit Your work in our lives.

Empower us as You did the Prophets of old; embolden us in our witness to our family, our neighbours and all whom we meet.

Fill us with Your Spirit
**All: That our faith might be enriched**
Fill us with Your Spirit
**All: That our lives might be empowered**
Fill us with Your Spirit
**All: That our witness might be emboldened**
Fill us with Your Spirit
**All: That Your name might be glorified**


'And if the Spirit of Him who raised Jesus from the dead is living in you,
He who raised Christ from the dead will also give life to your mortal
bodies through His Spirit, who lives in you.'          *(Rom 8:11)*

Show me Your ways, O Lord
**All: Teach me Your paths**
Guide me in Your truth and teach me
**All: For You are God my Saviour, and my hope is in You all day long**


Holy Spirit, without Your power in the Church today we shall always be
weak and ineffective in our mission.
How can the world see You through our lives if they cannot see the power
of Your love shining through?
How can the world feel Your healing touch if we do not know the reality
of Your presence in our lives?
How can we show a world that is searching where to find spiritual
fulfilment if our lives have not first been made whole?

Holy Spirit, Your creative breath is the power in Your Church today.
May we know that power in this place and in our lives.
**Amen**

# Wholeness

I will give you a new heart and put a new spirit within you; I will take the heart of stone out of Your flesh and give you a heart of flesh.    *Ezek 36:26*

Into the warmth of Your presence we come, Lord God

**All: With the offerings of our praise, our worship, our prayers and our lives.**

Into the warmth of Your presence we come, Lord God

**All: Freed from the distractions of the world, free to meditate on Your word.**

Into the warmth of Your presence we come, Lord God

**All: To be blessed by the depth of Your love and the warmth of this fellowship.**

It is good to be here, Lord; good to be in fellowship with each other; good to know the presence of Your Spirit in this place; good to know that You are here with us, listening, prompting, touching lives, healing, renewing, making us whole.

I will praise You, O Lord, among the nations;

**All: I will sing of You among the peoples**

For great is Your love, higher than the heavens

**All: Your faithfulness reaches to the skies**

Be exalted, O God, above the heavens

**All: And let Your glory be over all the earth.**

*(Psalm 108)*

In Your eyes, Father all are loved,
created in Your image,
a part of Your purpose,
of equal worth.
Forgive us that we have divided this world
into the 'have' and the 'have-nots',
into the rich and the poor,
the 'in crowd' and the outcasts,
members and non-members,
us and them

Forgive our insensitivity,
our selfishness,
our greed and pride

Help us to see others as You see them

We join together in the words of the Lord's Prayer

**All: Our Father...**

'Give to the LORD the glory due His name; Bring an offering, and come before Him.  Oh, worship the LORD in the beauty of holiness!'

*1 Chr 16:29*

Lord God, You breathed this world into being, and in Your infinite wisdom created mankind to be its stewards.

**All: Thank You, Creator God**

You created mankind in Your image, and wanted nothing more than to have fellowship with Your creation, Your family.

**All: Thank You, Father God**

When mankind had failed Your purpose, You did not discard us, but poured out Your love in the person of Jesus, Your Son; who came into this world that we might have life and have it to the full.

**All: Thank You, Loving God**

And now we stand before You, Your children; brothers and sisters of a heavenly Father, in a relationship made right again through the sacrificial love of Your dear Son upon a cross and His glorious Resurrection.

Shall we spend a moment or two in quiet reflection.
For love, freely given to all

*(pause)*

For wholeness, the healing touch for broken lives

*(pause)*

For Salvation, for being made right again with God

*(pause)*

And now with the angels in heaven we declare

**All: To Him who sits on the throne and to the Lamb
be praise and glory and honour and power, for ever and ever. Amen**

# Healing

Listen to the words of Jesus in Luke's Gospel:
"The Spirit of the Lord is upon me, because He has anointed me to preach good news to the poor. He has sent me to proclaim freedom for the prisoners and recovery of sight for the blind, to release the oppressed."

**All: "The Lord is my shepherd, I shall not be in want. He makes me lie down in green pastures, He leads me beside still waters, He restores my soul."**

This is the God we serve. A God of love, of healing and power.

**All: Alleluia**

This is the God we serve. A God who loves us with a Father's love.

**All: Alleluia**

A God who laughs as we laugh, and suffers as we suffer

**All: Alleluia**

A God whose touch brings not only healing but wholeness

**All: Alleluia**


Father God, let me never forget that in Your dear Son Jesus Christ You hung on a cross for me, and for all those who have gone before or who are yet to enter this dark world.
You suffered, bled and died in agony; and the agony that You bore that day encompassed the agony that we so often heap upon our own shoulders; our hopelessness, suffering, depression, disappointments, lost hopes and dreams.
You feel our pain.
Weep as we weep.
Hurt as we hurt.
You know more about us than we do ourselves and the sap that rises from the depth of Your love will always refresh, as in the vine that is damaged. And we shall show fruit again in Your time, and in eternity

**All: Teach me Your way, O Lord, and I will walk in Your truth; give me an undivided heart, that I may fear Your name.**

**I will praise You, O Lord my God, with all my heart; I will glorify Your name forever. For great is Your love toward me.** *(Psalm 86)*

Father, forgive our unbelief. Forgive us those times when we cry to You for mercy, for healing, for release and yet in our hearts expect so much less. Forgive us those times when we pray for a deluge and expect only drizzle.

Remind us of the power of Your Holy Spirit working through the lives of those early apostles; ordinary people doing extraordinary things for Your glory.

Remind us that Jesus healed all who came to him. That Jesus came to make broken lives whole.

Forgive us Father for our unbelief. Accept our mustard seed of faith, for that is often all we have to offer in times of sorrow or distress.

In a moment of quiet reflection we bring to God our incompleteness, our hurts, our pains, our fears and unbelief

*(silence)*

O Lord our Shepherd

**All: Lead me beside the still waters that restore my soul.**

O Lord our Saviour

**All: Give release from the fears, uncertainties and unease of this life.**

O Lord our healer

**All: Touch our lives as only You can touch them and flood them with the power of Your Spirit.**

In a moment of quiet reflection we remember the compassion, humility and selfless love shown by Jesus

*(silence)*

"My sheep know my voice, and I know them. They follow me, and I give them eternal life, so that they will never be lost. No one can snatch them out of my hand." *(John 10)*

This is the God we serve. A God who wants us to enjoy His presence; a God who brings wholeness and healing into lives that are incomplete.

**All: Alleluia!**

# Body

We meet today Lord as Your saints have met throughout the ages, wanting to offer You our sacrifice of praise and worship, wanting to grow together as the Body of Christ in this place, wanting to be here more than anywhere else.

"A body is made up of many parts, and each of them has its own use. That's how it is with us. There are many of us, but we each are part of the body of Christ, as well as part of one another."                    *Romans 12*

For each member of this worshipping fellowship.

**All: We thank You, Heavenly Father**

For the diversity of gifts and talents expressed within it.

**All: We thank You, Heavenly Father**

For those whose gifts have yet to be discovered.

**All: We thank You, Heavenly Father**

For those who consider themselves of little worth in this world but in Your eyes are of immeasurable value.

**All: We thank You, Heavenly Father**

For all who seek to serve You in this place and in this world, that Your love peace and grace might be seen in the simple actions of living.

**All: We thank You, Heavenly Father**

Father, it is our will to know You more, through the study of Your word; through worship and through prayer; through listening in the quieter moments of our lives.

**All: Forgive those times when our minds are distracted, when thoughts wander from You to the mundane aspects of our lives. When tensions and fears occupy our prayer time.**

Draw near to us in the difficult moments of our lives; enfold us with the warmth and security of Your love

**All: That we might know the peace and serenity of Your fellowship**

In a moment of quietness, we can allow our thoughts to centre on the Godhead; on God the Father, God the Son and God the Holy Spirit, united Three in One.

*(silence)*

In a moment of quietness we can reflect on our own worth in God's eyes, and the value of each member of this fellowship to the life of the body.

*(silence)*

In a moment of quietness we can pray for the building up of this body. For each member to understand his or her own gifting and talent, and for no one to think themselves more worthy than another.

*(silence)*

We join together in the words of the Lord's prayer

**All: Our Father...**

Father God, we are joined to You through the death and the Resurrection of Your Son, Jesus Christ. You held nothing back, endured not only a father's pain but the actual pain of that cross, so that we might know the true meaning and the potential cost of Love.
As You are One with the Holy Spirit and with Your Son may we also be one, united in the body which is Your Church here on earth.
As You so publicly demonstrated Your love through sacrifice, may we also offer the sacrifice of our lives in service in worship and in our daily lives.

'Dear friends, God is good. So I beg you to offer your bodies to Him as a living sacrifice, pure and pleasing. That's the most sensible way to serve God.'                                                                                      *Romans 12*

Joined together one with another, members of the same body and joint heirs with all those saints who have gone before, we proclaim

**All:  To Him who sits on the throne and to the Lamb, be praise and honour and glory and power, for ever and ever**

Joined together with one another and in fellowship with our Creator we proclaim our faith to the world, through our words and through our lives.

**ALL: Praise the Lord, all You nations; extol him, all You peoples. For great is His love towards us, and the faithfulness of the Lord endures forever. Praise the Lord!**

# Intercessory Prayer

'Now in the morning, having risen a long while before daylight, He went out and departed to a solitary place; and there He prayed.'

*(Mark 1:35)*

Jesus knew the importance of prayer, and it is obvious from the Gospel narrative that He prayed both for himself and others (Read John 17).

Within an act of worship it seems a natural extension of our prayer for it to flow from an act of adoration, confession or thanksgiving to one of love and concern for others and for situations beyond the walls within which we meet.

There are pitfalls which need avoiding - including the shopping list of requests read out at speed, or the assumption that our own needs are too trivial to concern the Almighty - and most of us have at some point drifted off to sleep during a particular slot of self-indulgent prayer, often accompanied I have found by lapses into sixteenth century language......
but I digress!

For a practical guide to intercessory prayer I would recommend wholeheartedly John Pritchard's excellent book *The Intercessions Handbook* (SPCK ISBN 0-281-04979-3) which covers the challenges and the problems of public intercessory prayer, and then goes on to discuss prayer in different situations - including all-age worship, small groups and personal prayer with lots of practical ideas for focussing prayer through the use of a variety of materials.

# Exploring Prayer

There are no hard and fast rules about prayer, merely guidelines - and the major one is that laid down by Jesus when asked by His own followers how they should pray:

> "And when you pray, do not use vain repetitions as the heathen do. For they think that they will be heard for their many words. Therefore do not be like them. For your Father knows the things you have need of before you ask Him.
>
> 'When you pray, say:
>
> Our Father in heaven,
>
> Hallowed be Your name.
>
> Your kingdom come.
>
> Your will be done
>
> On earth as it is in heaven.
>
> Give us day by day our daily bread.
>
> And forgive us our sins,
>
> For we also forgive everyone who is indebted to us.
>
> And do not lead us into temptation,
>
> But deliver us from the evil one.'"

Explore prayer using whatever materials are available, but use them sensitively. For thousands of years God's children have offered Him their prayers, and there is a wealth of wisdom and beauty within that tradition that should not be carelessly discarded but treasured - it links the saints of today with those who have gone before.
Having said that, prayer should always seek to be contemporary in the way that it links this generation to a God who is beyond history and time.

There should be a balance in our prayer life. But just as importantly, there should be life in our prayer.

## Acknowledgements

Prayers and responses which have no acknowledgement are of my own composition. Quotations and prayers credited to their original author can be found, among other places within the following publications.

Ward, Jennifer and Wild, Hannah, *The Lion Christian Quotation Collection*, (Lion 1997)
*The SPCK Book of Christian Prayer*, (SPCK 1995)

Other sources which I have found useful for research

Adam, David, *The Rhythm of Life*, (SPCK 1996)
Livingstone, Elizabeth A (editor), *The Concise Oxford Dictionary of the Christian Church*, (Oxford University Press 1977)
Metzer, Bruce E and Coogan, Michael D (editors), *The Oxford Companion to the Bible*, (Oxford University Press 1993)
Mitton, Michael, *Restoring the Woven Cord*, (Darton, Longman and Todd Ltd 1995)